# Time Is Money

*The Business Value of Web Performance*

Tammy Everts

Beijing · Boston · Farnham · Sebastopol · Tokyo   O'REILLY®

**Time Is Money**

by Tammy Everts

Printed in the United States of America.

Published by O'Reilly Media, Inc., 1005 Gravenstein Highway North, Sebastopol, CA 95472.

O'Reilly books may be purchased for educational, business, or sales promotional use. Online editions are also available for most titles (*http://safaribooksonline.com*). For more information, contact our corporate/institutional sales department: 800-998-9938 or *corporate@oreilly.com*.

| | |
|---|---|
| **Editor:** Brian Anderson | **Indexer:** Wendy Catalano |
| **Production Editor:** Nicholas Adams | **Interior Designer:** Monica Kamsvaag |
| **Copyeditor:** Jasmine Kwityn | **Cover Designer:** Randy Comer |
| **Proofreader:** Charles Roumeliotis | **Illustrator:** Rebecca Demarest |

June 2016:          First Edition

**Revision History for the First Edition**

2016-05-25:   First Release

See *http://oreilly.com/catalog/errata.csp?isbn=9781491928745* for release details.

978-1-491-92874-5

[LSI]

# Contents

# Introduction

If you know me, or if you've ever attended one of my talks or read any of my articles or blog posts (oh, so many blog posts!), then you know I'm fascinated by the impact of web performance on human behavior. (For the purposes of this book, let's use this simple definition of web performance: the speed and availability of web pages.) Because of the space in which I work, most of this human behavior gets correlated to business metrics. For the past six years, I've been corralling and writing about every case study I can get my hands on that documents this correlation.

In hindsight, it was probably inevitable that I should finally sit down and pull all these stories under one roof. I'm excited to bring these stories to you and hopefully make you a performance convert, if you aren't one already.

## Why Should Anyone Care About Web Performance?

Maybe you don't care about performance (yet). But chances are, no matter what kind of site you run—from retail to media to SaaS—you care about one or more of these metrics:

- Bounce rate
- Cart size
- Conversions
- Revenue
- Time on site
- Page views
- User satisfaction

- User retention
- Organic search traffic
- Brand perception
- Productivity
- Bandwidth/CDN savings

Are you targeting at least one of these metrics? Then you should also care about performance.

One thing I've learned over the years is that, if you can name a business metric, then you can map it to web performance in some quantifiable way. I have yet to find a metric that defied mapping. In fact, for me—and I know I'm not alone in this—the relationship between performance and online success has become so obvious that it comes as a bit of a surprise to encounter resistance to the idea. But there is definitely resistance out there—or, if not outright resistance, then at the very least a serious lack of education. Hence this book.

## My Hopes for This Book

One of the topics that comes up a lot in the web performance space is the challenge of convincing other people in your organization to care enough about performance that they're willing to invest some resources into fixing it. It's tough fighting for resources to fix a problem that, until recently, has been largely a silent killer. One of my goals in writing this book is to give all the performance converts out there the ammunition they need to put together a strong business case.

If you've been in this space for any length of time, you're probably familiar with some of the research and case studies—from Walmart to Aberdeen—that are mainstays of pretty much every speaker deck you encounter. These stories are great, and you'll find them covered here for the benefit of performance newcomers. But I've also cast my net wide to include stories that will, hopefully, be new to you.

Many of the case studies in this book focus on retail. That's because, particularly in the early years of studying web performance, those were the success stories that were easier to measure and tell. But in recent years we've seen performance stories from a variety of different verticals, including media, travel, SaaS, and even political sites. As our tools and metrics have evolved, so has our ability to gauge the impact of performance changes on people and businesses. I've spread my search to include as many of these diverse stories as I could track down (some of which were added hours before this book went into production!).

## Performance Is a Human Issue

When you finish this book, I'd love it if you walked away having internalized the fact that performance is very much a human issue.

We are incredibly lucky that we have the tools to measure and analyze how people use our sites and apps, but we shouldn't fall into the trap of reducing people to mere numbers on a dashboard. There are real people—millions upon millions of them—behind every study and statistic referenced in the pages ahead.

Ultimately, if we care about our businesses, then all those real actual human beings should be the first and last thing we think about every day.

# The Psychology of Web Performance

Before we dive into case studies, it's important to first understand the roots of our craving for lightning-fast online experiences.

Over the past 40-something years, there's been a great deal of fascinating research into how human beings engage with technology. These studies—many of which have findings that have persisted over the years—demonstrate that we don't just *want* our technology to be fast, but at a deep neurological level, we *need* it to be fast. And because these needs are deeply rooted in our neural wiring, they're unlikely to change, no matter how much we might wish they could.

## Fast Websites and Apps Create Happier Users

When users are happy as a result of a fast website, they're more likely to follow calls to action telling them to register, download, subscribe, request information, or purchase.

Unhappy users—those who experience a mere 2-second slowdown in how a web page loads—simply do less. They make almost 2% fewer queries, they click 3.75% less often, and they report being significantly less satisfied with their overall experience. Worse, they tell their friends about their negative experience.

A UK survey of 1,500 web users[1] found  that:

- 71% of people surveyed feel regularly inconvenienced by slow websites (Figure 1-1).

---

1 "Need for Speed," 1&1 Internet. 2011.

- Over 30% report that their performance-related stress or anger has *increased*, not decreased, over the years.

- 50% believe websites have either not improved in speed or have become slower over the past several years.

- 78% felt some kind of negative emotion due to slow or unreliable websites.

- Women (34%) are slightly more likely than men (27%) to report feeling stress or anger over slow web performance.

- 44% of users say that slow online transactions make them unsure about the success of the transaction.

- 42% of men and 35% of women have decided not to use a company again as a result of experiencing a slow website.

71% of people feel regularly inconvenienced by slow websites

*Figure 1-1. Results of the "Need for Speed" survey conducted by 1&1 Internet*

## How Fast Do We Expect Web Pages to Be?

We expect a lot from our online experiences. We want websites to be easy to use, we want them to be safe, and we want them to be fast. And when it comes to site speed, our demands are relentless. In 2006, the average online shopper expected pages to load in 4 seconds or less.[2] Today, 49% expect load times of 2 seconds or less, and 18%—one out of five—expect pages to load instantly (Figure 1-2).[3]

This shouldn't come as a surprise to anyone who's been tracking decades' worth of research into how humans use technology. (If you haven't been doing this, that's OK: I've got your back.) In lab test after lab test, going back as far as Robert B. Miller's classic research on human responses to computer perfor-

---

2 Akamai Technologies and Jupiter Research, 2006.

3 "2014 Consumer Web Performance Expectations Survey," Akamai Technologies.

mance,[4] studies have found that people are—and always have been—most comfortable, most efficient, and most productive with response times of less than 2 seconds.

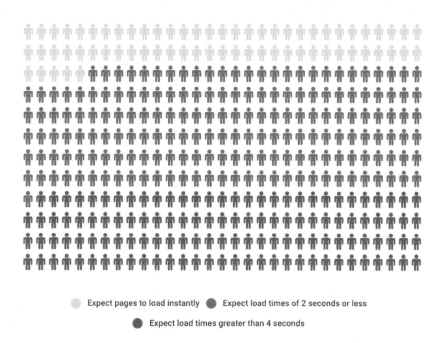

Expect pages to load instantly  Expect load times of 2 seconds or less
Expect load times greater than 4 seconds

*Figure 1-2. 49% of Internet users expect web pages to load in 2 seconds or less (Akamai)*

It's tempting to label ourselves picky and impatient, but we're not. There's a wealth of research into what happens to us at a neurological level when we're forced to deal with slow or interrupted processes. It isn't pretty.

---

4 Robert B. Miller, "Response Time in Man–Computer Conversational Transactions," 1968.

### It's About Neuroscience, Not Entitlement

Consider the following reader comments on *The New York Times* article "For Impatient Web Users, an Eye Blink Is Just Too Long to Wait":

> *Oh... pity the hyper-impatient web generation. Such busy lives with so many important things to do—like post the latest drivel onto their Facebook pages or download the YouTube viral video of the day. Oops, sorry—of the minute.*

> *Why oh why are these sites being flooded with people complaining about sites taking minutes to load, and others decrying the downfall of patience? This is about neuroscience and rhythm, not entitlement and overt frustration.*

## Our Need for Web Speed

Our perception of time varies according to many factors, including (but certainly not limited to) our age, our location, our emotions, and assorted external stimuli.

Not surprisingly, this inconsistency applies to our online experiences as well:

- The average web user perceives load times as being 15% slower than they actually are (Figure 1-3).

- Later, when recalling the experience, they remember load times as being 35% slower.[5]

- The average person believes they spend 9 minutes per day waiting for slow websites. This translates to two full days every year.[6] (I'm skeptical about this one. I spend a lot of time online, and even I don't believe I spend two days a year waiting for pages to load. But this stat is an interesting gauge of how people *feel* about the Web, even if it's not entirely accurate.)

---

5 Stoyan Stefanov, "Psychology of Performance," 2010.

6 "Need for Speed," 1&1 Internet, 2011.

- Adding indicators like spinners and progress bars can trick us into believing that pages are up to 10% faster than they actually are.[7]

Our perception of web speed is extremely unreliable both during and after an online experience

○ Actual  ● Perceived  ● Remembered

*Figure 1-3. The average web user perceives load times as being 15% slower than they actually are; later, they recall the experience as being 35% slower*

While what we *say* we expect from online experiences is inaccurate and highly variable, how we actually respond to different page speeds is much more consistent—and has been so for several decades.

Usability expert Jakob Nielsen has stated[8] that human responses to poor load times are based on two aspects of how our brains function:

*Our poor short-term memory*
Information stored in short-term memory decays quickly.

*Our need to feel in control*
Being forced to wait makes us feel powerless and frustrated.

According to Nielsen, 0.1 seconds gives us the illusion of instantaneous response, 1 second keeps our flow of thought seamless, and 10 seconds is

7 Colin Barras, "Visual tricks can make downloads seem quicker," New Scientist, 2010.

8 Jakob Nielsen, "Website Response Times," June 21, 2010.

enough to keep our attention—barely. After 10 seconds, our minds wander, making it harder to get back on task once a page finally loads (Figure 1-4).

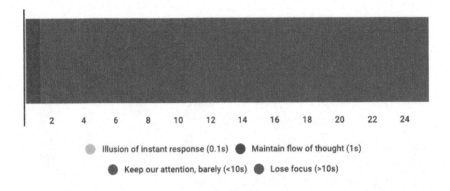

Figure 1-4. *According to research that has persisted since 1993, 0.1 seconds gives us the illusion of instantaneousness; after 10 seconds, we lose focus*

The Internet may change, and web pages may grow and evolve, but user expectations are constant. *The numbers about human perception and response times have been consistent for more than 45 years.* These numbers are hard-wired. We have zero control over them. They're consistent regardless of the type of device, application, or connection we're using at any given moment.

But why? This is where things get really interesting.

## Why Are We Impatient? Because Neuroscience

This section is for all the hardcore psychology geeks out there. If this isn't you, that's OK. Skip it. The main point I want you to take away is the knowledge that our impatience is an indelible part of our incredible human circuitry.

If you're still reading, then you may be interested in knowing that, at any given moment, there are three types of memory processing at work in your brain:

- Sensory memory
- Short-term memory
- Working memory

(There's also long-term memory, but it doesn't really come into play here.)

## SENSORY MEMORY

Every time you see something, this visual information is taken in by photoreceptor cells in your eyes and sent to the occipital lobe in your brain. This is your iconic memory. It's just one of your three types of sensory memories (the other two govern sound and touch).

People have been studying how iconic memory works for almost 300 years. In one of the earliest studies,[9] a glowing coal was attached to the wheel of a cart. The wheel was spun faster and faster until observers perceived an unbroken circle of light. The study concluded that the glowing coal had to perform a complete cycle in 100 milliseconds or less in order to create the illusion of a fiery circle. This early study identified the phenomenon we now call "persistence of vision," which is predicated on the fact that our iconic memory holds on to visual information for about 100 milliseconds. After that, the "memory store" runs out and the iconic memory needs to be refreshed with new visual information.

This number has remained consistent throughout the centuries. Interestingly, and perhaps not coincidentally, 100 milliseconds is Google's stated goal when it comes to page load times.

## 100 milliseconds

Google's goal for ideal load times

*We want you to be able to flick from one page to another as quickly as you can flick a page on a book. So we're really aiming very, very high here... at something like 100 milliseconds.*

**—URS HÖLZLE, SENIOR VICE PRESIDENT OF TECHNICAL INFRASTRUCTURE, GOOGLE**

9  Alan D. Baddely, *Human Memory: Theory and Practice*, 1990.

Iconic memory, along with the other two types of sensory memory, is primitive. We can't consciously choose what information is stored in it, and we can't will it to last longer. If we could, we'd probably go insane or accidentally walk in front of a bus.

Some sensory memory *does* stick, of course, provided it's used quickly and eventually consolidated into your long-term memory.

### SHORT-TERM MEMORY AND WORKING MEMORY

If our sensory memory's role is to provide comprehensive information on our entire sensory experience, it's our short-term memory's job to extract the relevant bits and throw them into the hopper of our working memory. Your short-term memory can store information for 10–15 seconds, at most—just enough time for your working memory to process, manipulate, and control it.

So the goal in getting page load times down to 100 milliseconds is to keep information from falling through the cracks in our iconic memory, while also giving our short-term and working memory ample time to do all the parsing they need to do before they start losing information.

## What Is "Flow" and How Does It Relate to How We Use the Web?

For hundreds of thousands of years, human beings have evolved to perform actions in beautiful, sequential flows. Our day-to-day tasks—building a fire, hunting antelope, baking bread, milking a cow—have been comprised of a series of minute actions that flow more or less seamlessly into the next.

In *Finding Flow: The Psychology of Engagement with Everyday Life* (Basic Books, 1998), noted psychology researcher Mihaly Csíkszentmihályi observed that people who perform seamless, sequence-based activities on a regular basis are happier than people who don't. He coined the term "flow" to describe this state of being.

It's only in the past 40 years, with the advent of computers, that we've imposed a new set of demands on our brains. As most of us are painfully aware, instead of offering a series of smoothly sequential actions, computer use is characterized by lag, downtime, and restarts. Our flow-oriented brains simply aren't wired to deal with the fits and starts of human–computer interaction.

In my travels, I encounter people who are skeptical about the impact of lag, downtime, and restarts on productivity and other key performance indicators. The argument I hear is that most people do, in fact, adjust to poor performance.

As it turns out, these people may be somewhat correct, but they may also be focusing on the wrong part of the picture.

## Questioning Our Assumptions: Do Delays Really Hurt Productivity?

In a 1999 study into workplace interruptions,[10] groups of workers were subjected to various disruptions in the course of their day-to-day responsibilities. They were then measured in terms of both their productivity and their self-reported state of mind. While this study focused on general workplace interruptions, with only some attention given to human–computer interaction, there were some fascinating findings that are arguably relevant to web performance:

*Finding 1: Participants developed strategies that let them deal effectively with interruptions and maintain their productivity*

> This research suggests that, at least for some workers in some environments, not only do they learn how to cope with interruptions, they may even strive to overcompensate for their potential performance decline.

*Finding 2: However, this coping mechanism is achieved at the expense of higher psychological costs*

> Cumulatively, interruptions had a negative impact on emotions and well-being. In addition, participants ultimately needed to increase the amount of effort required to perform the same tasks.

*Finding 3: Over time, interruptions affected participants' ability and willingness to resume work and take on new tasks*

> Interruptions seemed to have a cumulative effect. When the number of interruptions grew, the resumption time (i.e., the time needed to restart the task) became disproportionately longer. The participants seemed to lose motivation and develop mental fatigue.

## What Does This Mean in Web Performance Terms?

When dealing with application delays, it's possible that people can develop coping strategies that allow them to maintain productivity in the short term. But the missing ingredient here is flow. And without flow, eventually our sense of motivation and well-being suffers.

---

10  Mary Czerwinski, Eric Horvitz, and Susan Wilhite, "A Diary Study of Task Switching and Interruptions," Microsoft Research, 1999.

It's also important to remind ourselves that application performance is just one part of the greater world. Our everyday lives are filled with events—from sitting in traffic to standing in line at the grocery store—that challenge our need for flow. Poor web performance is just one problem, but for those of us who spend much of our work and personal time online, it's extra friction in an already friction-filled world. Its effects are cumulative, as most of us aren't capable of compartmentalizing our stress.

## Web Stress: It's a Thing

When websites perform poorly, we react badly (there's even some research that suggests using slow websites increases our blood pressure!). This is not surprising given what we now know about our deep craving for flow.

In 2011, CA Technologies commissioned Foviance, a customer experience consultancy, to conduct a series of lab experiments at Glasgow Caledonian University.[11] The participants wore an EEG (electroencephalography) cap to monitor their brainwave activity while they performed routine online transactions. Participants completed tasks using either a 5 MB web connection or a connection that had been artificially slowed down to 2 MB.

Brainwave analysis from the experiment revealed that participants had to concentrate up to 50% more when using websites via the slower connection. When asked what they liked most and least about the websites they used during the study, participants frequently cited speed as a top concern:

> *The website was very slow, so it took a really long time to load the book preview.*

> *What I liked least about the site is its speed.*

The study also found that people were most likely to experience the greatest levels of stress during two points in the transaction process:

*Search*
    Finding and selecting products

*Checkout*
    Entering personal information and concluding the sale

---

11  "Web Stress: A Wake Up Call for European Business," Foviance (for CA Technologies), February 2010.

Intuitively, this makes sense. Searching for an item already comes with an inherent amount of stress, as most of us are concerned with finding the right item at the best possible price. And the checkout process—when we hand over our personal and credit card information—is fraught with a certain amount of stress as well. Add page slowdowns to the mix and it's easy to understand why the online shopping experience can become unpleasant.

## Mobile Users Feel Web Stress, Too

Mobile users are unhappy, too. According to an Akamai survey,[12] 39% of mobile users are dissatisfied with their online experiences, citing page slowdowns and site crashes as their top two complaints. More than half have experienced problems when using their phones or tablets, and 46% say they won't return to a site that performs badly (Figure 1-5).

Figure 1-5. According to Akamai research, many mobile users are dissatisfied with the performance of the sites they visit

---

12 "2014 Consumer Web Performance Expectations Survey," Akamai Technologies.

## What Does This Dissatisfaction with Mobile Performance Look Like at a Neuroscientific Level?

Based on the desktop neuroscientific research conducted by CA Technologies, Radware conducted a similar study in 2013, this time focusing on users of mobile devices.[13] (Disclosure: I worked for Radware at the time and directed this research.) Radware's study involved using a groundbreaking combination of eye-tracking and electroencephalography (EEG) technologies to monitor neural activity in a group of mobile users who were asked to perform a series of online transactions via mobile devices.

In the study, participants were asked to complete standardized shopping tasks on four ecommerce sites while using a smartphone. Some participants were served pages at normal speeds over WiFi, while others were served pages at a consistently slowed-down speed (using software that created an artificial 500-millisecond network delay). The participants didn't know that speed was a factor in the tests; rather, they believed that they were participating in a generic usability/brand perception study.

Some highlights of the study's findings:

- Users experienced frustration peaks of up to 26% at critical points.
- Like the CA Technologies study, frustration peaks were most common during the browsing and checkout phases.
- Faster pages correlated with increased user engagement (that's a good thing!).
- Slowness affected the entire perception of the brand, even nonperformance aspects of the site such as content, design, and navigation.
- Users experienced "web stress" even under ideal mobile browsing conditions.

---

13 "Mobile Web Stress: The Impact of Network Speed on Emotional Engagement and Brand Perception," Radware, 2013.

## "Phone Rage"

A survey by Harris Interactive for Tealeaf found that when we suffer from mobile performance issues, 11% of us confess to yelling at our phones, 23% of us curse at them, and 4% actually throw them (here's hoping the replacement phone performs better!)

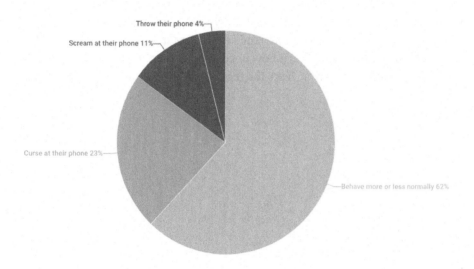

When mobile sites perform badly, we don't always handle it gracefully

## Takeaway

There's a fascinating disconnect between what we say we want and what, deep down, we really *need* from our online experiences. Over the past dozen or so years, user surveys have revealed that what we claim to want changes over time—from 8-second load times back in 1999 to 4 seconds in 2006 to around 2 seconds today. If we were to believe these surveys, then we'd conclude that we're an increasingly hasty, impatient species. We might be tempted to judge (or pity) ourselves as victims of our frantic modern lives.

But neuroscientific research—which studies how we actually think, not how we believe we think—tells a very different story. Over the decades, researchers have reproduced the same results: that, by and large, we function at our happiest best when our websites and apps (and technology in general) respond in fractions of a second. We may learn how to adapt to slower response times, but this adaptation will always (or at least for the foreseeable future) be awkward and uneasy.

# 2

# Speed as Competitive Advantage

In the United States alone, ecommerce has grown at an average rate of 15% year over year for the past five years. In 2014, online sales blew past the $300 billion threshold for the first time. By 2018, that number is projected to surpass the $400 billion mark (Figure 2-1).

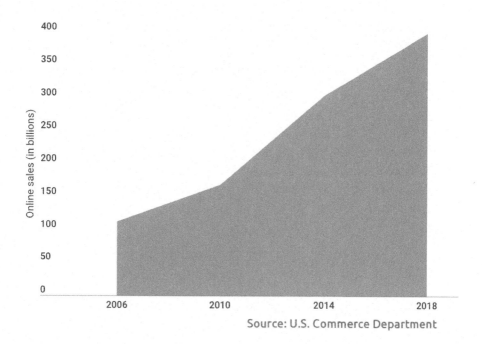

Source: U.S. Commerce Department

*Figure 2-1. By 2018, ecommerce in the US is projected to hit $400 billion per year*

As most of us know, however, all that money isn't just lying on a table waiting to be scooped up. The online marketplace has become a crowded, hypercompetitive space, and site owners are on constant lookout for anything that will give their websites an advantage. Site speed isn't always top of mind for many, but optimizing page load times is arguably the most straightforward way to differentiate a site from the competition.

*In user survey after user survey, site speed has emerged as one of the greatest factors in determining an individual's satisfaction with a website (second only to security).* Almost half of all online shoppers say they will abandon a page that takes more than 2 seconds to load.

In a traditional brick-and-mortar scenario, abandoning one store for another requires leaving the outlet and physically travelling to the waiting arms of the competition. On the Web, competitors are just a couple of clicks away.

---

*Two hundred and fifty milliseconds, either slower or faster, is close to the magic number for competitive advantage on the Web.*

**—HARRY SHUM, EXECUTIVE VP OF TECHNOLOGY AND RESEARCH, MICROSOFT**

---

For mobile, 74% of users say that 5 seconds is the maximum amount of time they'll wait before abandoning a page.[1] When those disappointed users bounce, most say a competing site is their next stop. And 46% say they will never return to the slow site.

---

1 "What Users Want from Mobile," Equation Research (for Gomez), 2011.

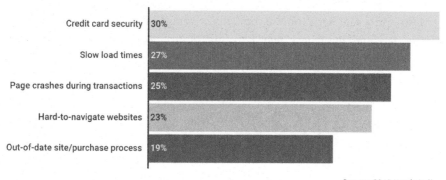

Source: 2015 Harris Poll

*Figure 2-2. Online shoppers' top 5 web performance frustrations*

These numbers clearly show that strong performance confers a competitive advantage online, but to what extent? What's the performance "sweet spot" (i.e., the ideal load time that will yield the best possible impact on your bottom line)?

## Retail Isn't the Only Vertical Market Affected by Performance

A great deal of attention is placed on retail performance because retail metrics are easy to capture: it's relatively short work to draw a line between load times and revenue. But performance affects other verticals as well. Media, travel, finance... if there are real people using your service online, then those people's behavior is susceptible to changes wrought by faster or slower web pages. I have yet to encounter a business that, after gathering enough user data and identifying the right metrics, didn't find a correlation between performance and their business.

I'll spend the rest of this chapter demonstrating how page speed has a measurable impact on every business metric you care about: brand perception, conversions, revenue, shopping cart abandonment, page views, and search engine ranking. But before we dive into that, I want to explore a question I frequently get asked...

## Slow Time Versus Downtime: Which Hurts Your Business More?

In 2013, Amazon.com famously went down for somewhere between 20 to 45 minutes (reports vary—after all, this *is* the Internet). That short failure came with a massive price tag. Based on the company's average sales volume of $117,882 per minute, *a 40-minute outage may have cost the company almost $5 million* (see Figure 2-3).

 **117,882**

Average loss in sales volume for each minute Amazon.com is down

*Figure 2-3. At Amazon, a 40-minute outage can cost the company almost $5 million*

Just a few days earlier, in an unrelated outage, Google's home page briefly went offline, *costing the company more than half a million dollars in lost ad revenue in just five minutes.*

High-profile outages and million-dollar losses grab headlines. They also scare the wits out of site owners. After all, there's no such thing as 100% uptime. Every site goes down eventually. The question isn't "Will my site go down?" The questions are "When will my next outage happen?" and "How long will it last?" and "How much will it cost me?"

With potential site failure hanging over their heads like the sword of Damocles, it's no surprise that contingency planning for downtime ranks high on site executives' lists of priorities. As it should. But with so much focus on spectacular, headline-grabbing outages, is it possible that site owners are missing the more silent—but equally deadly—problem of performance slowdowns?

### Our Perception of Outage-Related Risk May Be Out of Proportion to the Actual Risk

*Whether it's a public website or an internal web-based application, most of us believe that a successful DoS/DDoS attack results in a service outage. However, our Security Industry Sur-*

*vey... uncovered that the biggest impact of DoS/DDoS attacks in 2013 was service level degradation, which in most cases is felt as service slowness.*

**—2013 GLOBAL APPLICATION AND NETWORK SECURITY
REPORT, RADWARE**

---

Let's do the math.

According to a TRAC Research survey of 300 companies,[2] the average revenue loss for an hour of downtime was $21,000. For the same set of companies, average revenue loss due to an hour of performance slowdown (which was defined as response times exceeding 4.4 seconds) was much less (just $4,100).

Looking at these two sets of numbers, outages seem like a bigger source of concern. But wait. According to the same survey, website slowdowns occurred ten times more frequently than outages. In other words, according to this research, *slow-loading pages ultimately have twice the impact on revenue that site failures do.*

Revenue isn't the only metric that is affected quite differently by outages versus slowdowns. In one of the only studies (if not, the only study) into the impact of outages versus slowdowns on abandonment rates, Akamai found that sites that went down experienced, on average, a permanent abandonment rate of 9%. Sites that suffered from slow performance experienced a 28% permanent abandonment rate—an increase of more than 200% (Figure 2-4).[3]

### Permanent abandonment rate

| Outage | Slow performance |
|--------|------------------|
| 9% | 28% |

Source: Akamai

*Figure 2-4. Performance slowdowns result in abandonment rates that are more than 200% higher than outages (source: Akamai)*

---

2  Kevin Godskind and Bojan Simic, "Online Performance Is Business Performance," TRAC Research (for AlertSite), 2010.

3  Akamai, "The Impact of Web Performance on E-Retail Success," 2004.

*Downtime is better for a B2C web service than slowness. Slowness makes you hate using the service. Downtime you just try again later.*

**—LENNY RACHITSKY, PRODUCT MANAGER, AIRBNB**

## Brand Perception

First impressions matter, and they happen faster than you might think. According to one study, just 50 milliseconds—one-twentieth of a second—is all it takes for us to form an opinion about a website. And once we've formed that opinion, it colors how we feel about a site's credibility and usability, ultimately affecting whether or not we choose to make a purchase on that site. Creating a site that is both visually appealing and high performing can be a ticket to online success.

*The real thing we are after is to create a user experience that people love and they feel is fast... and so we might be frontend engineers, we might be dev, we might be ops, but what we really are is perception brokers.*

**—STEVE SOUDERS, AUTHOR, *HIGH PERFORMANCE WEB SITES***

## Slow Web Pages Undermine Brand Health

In the previous chapter, I cited neuroscientific research by Radware, in which mobile users were asked to complete transactions on an ecommerce site. Some participants experienced normal speeds, and some experienced load times that were artificially throttled with a 500-millisecond network delay. Participants didn't know that speed was a factor in the tests. Instead, they believed they were participating in a standard usability/brand perception study.

After each set of tests in the study, researchers conducted exit interviews with the subjects, who were asked to give their general impressions of each site and company. The adjectives for each exit interview were poured into a word cloud generator, which generated a cloud for each version (normal and slow) of each site. The results were revealing.

While both word clouds contained positive and negative descriptors for each site, the word cloud for the slower site contained *almost three times* more negative adjectives than the faster site. The adjectives associated with the site shifted from mainly easy-to-use (for the normal site) to a range of negative associations (for the slow version)—solely because of the page delays.

Some participants clearly picked up on the slight deterioration in performance (calling the slower site "slow" and "sluggish"), but those who used the slower site also developed negative perceptions of areas unrelated to speed. They reported that the site also seemed "boring," "inelegant," "clunky," "tacky," and "hard to navigate."

In other words, slower page loads affected people's perception of three important aspects of the site that are completely unrelated to load time:

- Content ("boring")
- Visual design ("tacky" and "confusing")
- Ease of navigation ("frustrating" and "hard to navigate")

---

*If a site is slow, people think it's broken. A slow website damages your brand.*

**—KENT ALSTAD, VICE PRESIDENT, ACCELERATION, RADWARE**

---

## CASE STUDY: HEALTHCARE.GOV'S "EPIC FAIL" IS CONFLATED WITH THE ENTIRE OBAMA ADMINISTRATION

In 2013, the United States conducted an ambitious overhaul of its healthcare system—the Affordable Care Act—which culminated in the launch of a new online service: Healthcare.gov. In October of 2013, American citizens were directed to the website to log on and create accounts. In the first two days, more than two million people accessed the site. Many of those early users experienced errors and delays that, not surprisingly, drew a lot of media attention.[4]

---

4 Steven Brill, "Code Red," Time Magazine, March 10, 2014.

While some of the site's performance problems were attributed to unexpected traffic load (the site was reportedly never tested for scalability and performance before launch), audits of the pages themselves revealed a number of frontend problems ranging from JavaScript issues (too many files, many of which were unoptimized) and poorly performing third-party widgets and web fonts.

> *[The Healthcare.gov launch] plays into the suspicion that resides in really all Americans that, outside of narrow functions they can see and appreciate, like Social Security and national parks, the government just can't get it done.*
>
> **—AUSTAN GOOLSBEE, ECONOMIC ADVISOR TO THE OBAMA**
> **PRESIDENTIAL CAMPAIGN**

After much finger pointing, HealthCare.gov was eventually retooled and its performance issues were largely resolved, but not before it had inflicted serious brand damage—not just to the Affordable Care Act, but to President Barack Obama's second term in office.

Articles appeared in publications such as *The New Yorker, The Wall Street Journal, Harvard Business Review, The Guardian,* and *Bloomberg Businessweek* (along with the now infamous cover depicting a partially loaded image of Obama accompanied by a spinner icon). While not all the coverage was negative, many journalists and pundits took advantage of a ripe opportunity to conflate Healthcare.gov's "epic fail" with the system itself, as well as with Obama's administration.

Was this fair or accurate? Arguably no. But performance is an entrenched aspect of how a brand is perceived. Fairness doesn't come into play.

## Conversions and Revenue

Conversions are the lifeblood of your retail or SaaS business. Improving how pages perform is arguably one of the single greatest ways site owners can optimize their sites' conversion rates. This has been proven beyond a shadow of a doubt by a massive body of research—from SMBs to SaaS vendors to retail giants

—that demonstrates the correlation between page speed, conversions, and ultimately revenue.

**CASE STUDY: EVERY 1 SECOND OF LOAD TIME IMPROVEMENT EQUALS A 2% CONVERSION RATE INCREASE FOR WALMART.COM**

The people at WalmartLabs (a technology incubator under the Walmart umbrella) knew that Walmart.com was suffering from performance issues. As a for instance, initial measurement showed that an item page took about 24 seconds to load for the slowest 5% of users. Why? The usual culprits: too many page elements, slow third-party scripts, multiple hosts (25% of page content was served by third parties), and various performance no-nos.

WalmartLabs dedicated a scrum team to one sprint of performance optimization. At the start of the process, the team performed some baseline measurements in which they used their real user monitoring (RUM) data to gather load time data for key pages and look for patterns. Then the team created targets for page performance, and at the end of the sprint, measured the impact of optimization on key metrics.[5]

Their findings showed a strong correlation between performance and conversions:

- Overall, converted shoppers were served pages that loaded twice as quickly as pages served to nonconverted shoppers.

- This trend persisted, even on individual pages that experienced greater load times.

- Nonbuyers were served category pages that were 2–3 seconds slower than category pages served to buyers.

- For every 1 second of improvement to load time, the site experienced up to a 2% improvement in conversion rate.

- For every 100 milliseconds of improvement, they grew incremental revenue by up to 1% (Figure 2-5).

---

5 Cliff Crocker, Aaron Kulick, and Balaji Ram, "Real User Monitoring at Walmart.com: A Story in Three Parts," 2012.

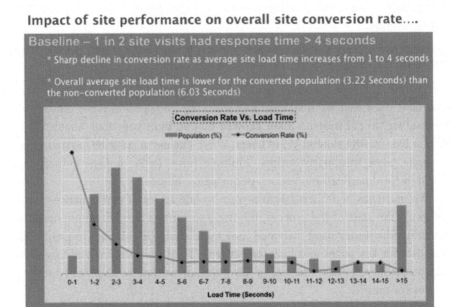

*Figure 2-5. Walmart web performance optimization case study*

## CASE STUDY: STAPLES.COM SHAVES 1 SECOND FROM LOAD TIME, IMPROVES CONVERSION RATE BY 10%

Providing an excellent customer experience is a stated goal at Staples.com, and the company knows that speed is an essential user experience ingredient. Knowing that you can't manage what you can't measure, the performance engineering team added real user monitoring to its measurement toolkit and began to immediately collect and graph data about real user experiences.

Using real user data, Staples saw an early relationship between load time and conversions. Conversion rate peaked between 3 and 4 seconds. After that, as load time increased, conversion rates decreased.

Following this finding, Staples developed and implemented an optimization process that involved a cross-functional team from business and marketing to engineering and analytics. The team's efforts included wrangling excessive third-party calls and taking an aggressive approach to image optimization. (Third parties and images are low-hanging fruit on the optimization tree, as they represent arguably the single greatest potential point of failure, considering that pages and images comprise roughly two-thirds of the average web page.)

As a result of these efforts, the team shaved a full second off of Staples.com's home page median load time, improving the site's conversion rate by roughly 10%.[6]

### CASE STUDY: AUTOANYTHING.COM CUTS PAGE LOAD IN HALF, INCREASES CONVERSION RATE BY 9%

Auto accessories retailer AutoAnything was challenged by the need to give shoppers a dynamic, rich-content online experience that also delivered a fast, reliable user experience. Despite already using a content delivery network (to shorten server round-trips and render pages faster), the website's home page took up to 10 seconds or longer to load. The site also suffered from a high shopping cart abandonment rate.

The retailer worked aggressively to cut page load times in half. With no other changes to the site, this performance improvement resulted in a 9% increase in conversion rate, an 11% increase in average cart size, and a 12%–13% increase in sales.[7]

---

*When you affect conversion by 9%, that is very significant on an annual basis.*

**—PARAG PATEL, CTO, AUTOANYTHING**

---

### CASE STUDY: MOZILLA SHAVES 2.2 SECONDS FROM LOAD TIMES, INCREASES DOWNLOAD CONVERSIONS BY 15.4%

In 2010, Mozilla made the painful realization that the entire landing page for Chrome loaded before the header for the Firefox landing page rendered. They also realized that load time might be a factor in download conversions. To improve performance, they focused on two things: combining (or removing) JavaScript files and inlining CSS files.

---

6 Cliff Crocker and Steve Skroce, "How to Measure Revenue in Milliseconds," 2014.

7 "AutoAnything Cuts Page Load Time in Half and Revs Up Sales by 13%," Radware, 2010.

After implementing these changes in an A/B test, Mozilla saw impressive results. Previously, they had predicted that a 1-second reduction in page load time would improve download conversions by 2.7%. In reality, their optimized experimental variation shaved 2.2 seconds off the average page load time and increased download conversions by 15.4%. With 275,000 daily visitors, they projected that this 15% improvement would translate to 10.28 million additional Firefox downloads per year.[8]

---

*Previously, we predicted a 1-second reduction in page load speed would improve download conversions by 2.7%. In reality, our optimized experimental variation shaved 2.2 seconds off the average page load time and increased download conversions by 15.4%!*

**—BLAKE CUTLER, SENIOR DATA ANALYST, MOZILLA**

---

## CASE STUDY: OBAMA FUNDRAISING PLATFORM IMPROVED SPEED BY 60% AND RAISED AN ADDITIONAL $34 MILLION

The fundraising stakes were high during the 2011–2012 US election season. The Obama campaign's goal was to raise $1 billion—an aggressive target.

---

*We knew from the very beginning that our new donation platform needed to be as fast as we could reasonably make it. We were very familiar with all the stories from huge companies like Amazon and Google about how only 100 milliseconds of latency can affect conversions by as much as 1%. Needless to say, performance was was one of our very top priorities.*

**—KYLE RUSH, DEPUTY DIRECTOR OF FRONTEND WEB DEVELOPMENT, OBAMA FOR AMERICA**

---

8 Blake Cutler, "Firefox and Page Load Speed, Part II," April 5, 2010.

With a tight timeline for creating a fast new donation platform, the campaign's web team made a few quick wins by plucking some low-hanging fruit, such as serving static HTML pages via a content delivery network. (A CDN stores static page assets in a network of edge caches, shortening the round-trip time required to deliver those assets to the user's browser.) The team also worked to ensure that the platform was stable enough to handle fundraising surges that accompanied major media events.

As a result of these optimizations (illustrated in Figure 2-6), the fundraising platform performed 60% faster. A/B testing revealed that, initially, the faster pages experienced a 14% increase in donation conversions. By the end of the campaign, the donation conversion rate was lifted by 49%. The campaign exceeded its fundraising goal, ultimately raising $1.1 billion.[9]

*Figure 2-6. After being optimized for performance, the Obama fundraising platform performed 60% faster and experienced a 14% increase in donation conversions*

9 Kyle Rush, "Meet the Obama campaign's $250 million fundraising platform," November 27, 2012.

**CASE STUDY: INTUIT CUTS LOAD TIMES BY MORE THAN HALF, INCREASES CONVERSIONS BY 14%**

In 2012, Intuit began an ambitious project: aggressively optimizing 50 pages from six of its marketing sites.[10] The imperative for the project came when the company's web team realized that average load times for its pages ranged from 12 to 15 seconds.

> There were a lot of negative things that came as a result of poor performance. Our users' experience, SEO, our page views were down, conversions were down. Worst of all, it was just embarrassing.
>
> We knew something had to be done. Engineering presented a case... but nobody got it. We just couldn't get people to buy in. Everybody was too busy, nobody had any time, nobody had resources. This changed one day. We had a frustrated engineer who, on his own time, started to optimize some of our pages. We had a successful A/B test that showed that faster pages actually improved our metrics. All of a sudden, the conversation went from "We're not interested" to "Hey, how fast can we optimize everything?"
>
> **—JAY HUNG, CHIEF ARCHITECT, WEBMOCHA (FOR INTUIT)**

The team's goal was to deliver a 50% improvement—taking average load times down to 6 seconds. They focused on implementing performance best practices, ranging from optimizing images to eliminating unnecessary beacons to ensuring their CDN was properly configured.

The team met its goal in the first six months. As a result, the site enjoyed measurable benefits to the business—chiefly, improved conversion rates. This inevitably led to the question: can we get even faster?

---

10 Norberth Danson and Jay Hung, "From Slow To Fast: Improving Performance On Intuit Web Sites By Up To 5x," 2013.

*The question of the day was: what would be the potential business upside if we got closer to, or under, 4 seconds. The situation was drastically different from a few months before. We weren't begging them to do performance optimizations. It was the other way around. They were coming to us and asking us to make things faster. We decided to aim for 2 seconds, just to see if we could do it.*

**—NORBERTH DANSON, SENIOR SOFTWARE ENGINEER, INTUIT**

After six more months of aggressive optimization, average load times shrank to an enviable 2–3 seconds, and conversions in key transactions had improved by up to 14% (see Figure 2-7). Their takeaway was that, for every 1 second of performance improvement, the site experienced up to a 3% improvement in conversion rate.

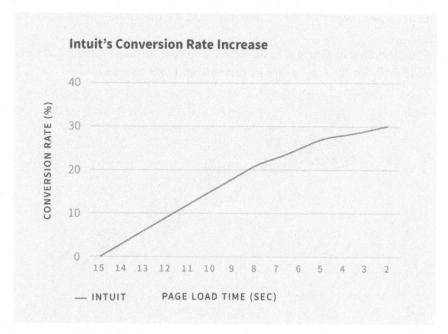

*Figure 2-7. Intuit found that for every 1 second of performance improvement, the site experienced up to a 3% improvement in conversion rate*

## Who Converts When?

If you've just read the previous pages, you may find yourself feeling mildly pan-icky, especially if you work on a site that serves thousands—or hundreds of thou-sands—of pages to visitors from around the world. You might be wondering, *How the heck do I optimize all my pages for all those visitors?* Fortunately, if you have access to real user data for your site, you can identify where to focus your optimization efforts.

## Different Pages in the Conversion Funnel Can Have Different Conversion Rates

When pages get slower, conversion rates suffer. But some types of pages suffer more than others. SOASTA, a performance testing and analytics provider, looked at real-life performance data for one of its ecommerce customers and found that, while slower load times correlated to fewer conversions, the impact was most dramatic when pages in the "browsing" part of the conversion funnel were slower.

As illustrated in Figure 2-8, the conversion rate shrinks by about 50% when the load time for "browse" pages increases from 1 to 6 seconds.

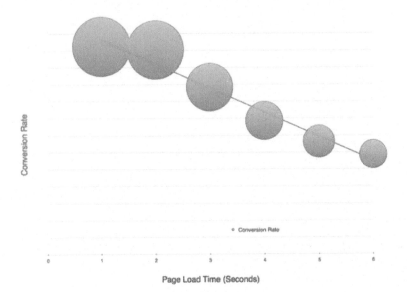

*Figure 2-8. When "browse" pages in a transaction path slow down, there's a dramatic impact on conversions*

And looking at the same set of user data from SOASTA (Figure 2-9), you can see that the impact on conversion rate is much less when checkout pages degrade in speed.

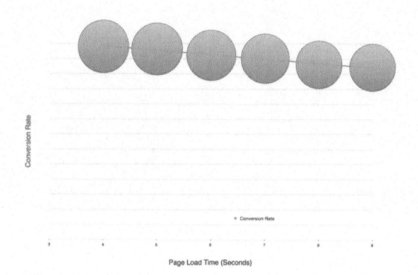

*Figure 2-9. When "checkout" pages slow down, conversions are much less affected*

## People Are More Patient with Specialty Sites Than with General Merchandisers

SOASTA also looked at data from two ecommerce sites: one of which sells specialty goods and the other of which sells general merchandise. They discovered that when pages slow down, both bounce rate and conversions suffer much more for the general merchandise retailer than for the specialty shop (see Figure 2-10 and Figure 2-11).

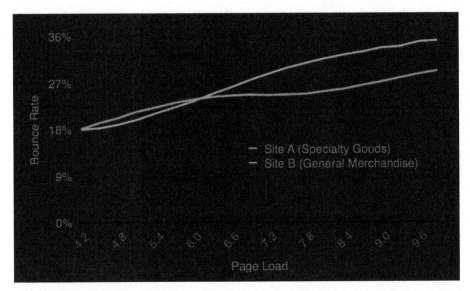

*Figure 2-10. When page load times slow down, bounce rate suffers more for general merchandise sites than for sites that sell specialty goods*

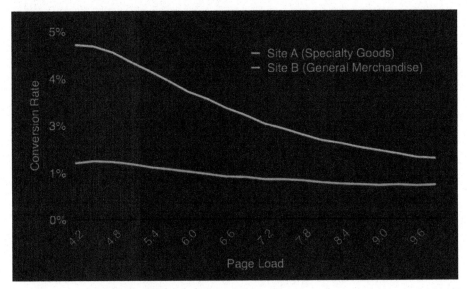

*Figure 2-11. When pages slow down, general merchandisers suffer even greater hits to their conversion rates than to their bounce rates*

## Visitors in Some Countries Are More Patient Than Visitors in Others

And finally, breaking down user data by geography, SOASTA found that when faced with slower load times, people in Australia were much less likely to bounce than visitors in the United States—possibly due to the fact that Australians are accustomed to suffering from slow performance across the board (see Figure 2-12).

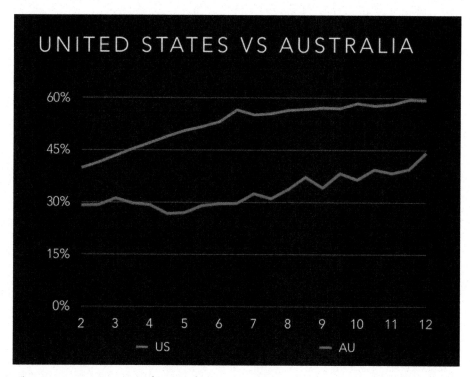

*Figure 2-12. Internet users in the United States are significantly more likely to bounce from slow sites than users in Australia*

## Shopping Cart Abandonment

Though numbers vary throughout the year, roughly 70% of online shopping carts are abandoned before checkout.

In recent years, more online retailers have begun to focus on accelerating their key landing pages and product pages. Many, however, are still neglecting their checkout process, to their detriment: 18% of shoppers say they'll abandon their cart if pages are too slow. This correlates to more than $3 billion in lost sales (across US ecommerce sites) due to poor performance.

Shopping cart speed doesn't just affect the current transaction, but potential future transactions as well: 46% of online shoppers cite checkout speed as the number one factor that determines whether or not they will visit a site again.[11]

## CASE STUDY: IMPACT OF PAGE SLOWDOWN ON SHOPPING CART ABANDONMENT

In 2011, Strangeloop worked with a customer who wanted to experiment with the impact of page slowdown on a five-step transaction.[12] They conducted a split test in which traffic was divided into three groups and each group was delivered a different user experience:

- Group 1 (the baseline) experienced a fully optimized transaction.
- Group 2 experienced a 2-second delay to just one page (page 3) of the transaction.
- Group 3 also experienced a 2-second delay to just one page, but in this case it was page 1 of the transaction (Figure 2-13).

The study found that just a 2-second delay in load time during a transaction resulted in abandonment rates of up to 87%.

---

11  "Case Study: Understanding the Impact of Slow Load Times on Shopping Cart Abandonment," Radware, 2013.

12  Joshua Bixby, "Slow Shopping Cart Pages Are Killing Conversions," Unbounce Blog, November 29, 2011.

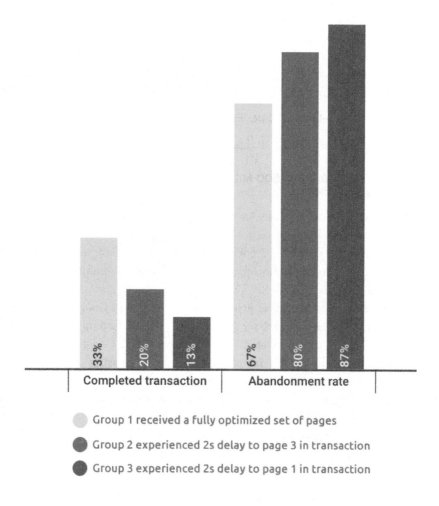

*Figure 2-13. Just a 2-second delay in load times during a transaction results in abandonment rates of up to 87%*

## Page Views and Bounce Rate

Page views and  bounce rate are both great indicators of customer engagement. Happy, engaged users view more pages, stay longer, and generally do more. Dissatisfied users abandon sites early and seldom return.

*We ran this experiment on mobile web where we added 160 kilo-bytes of hidden images, meaning the user saw nothing different. We just dumped a bunch of hidden images onto the page and increased page weight by 160 kilobytes. It triggered a 12% increase in bounce rate. Insane. Twelve percent is a lot of percent.*

**—LARA HOGAN, SENIOR ENGINEERING MANAGER, ETSY**

## CASE STUDY: AT GOOGLE, A 500-MILLISECOND SLOWDOWN EQUALED A 25% DECREASE IN SEARCHES

It's safe to say that Google is obsessed with speed. As discussed in the previous chapter, the company has a stated goal of delivering pages in 100 milliseconds or less. And later in this chapter, I'll cover page speed as a ranking factor in Google search results. So it comes as no surprise that the company monitors the impact of its own site changes.

Back in 2006, Marissa Mayer (who at the time served as Google's Vice President of Search Products and User Experience) shared findings from several experiments Google had conducted.[13] In one experiment, Google responded to user demand for more search results per page by increasing the number of results from 10 per page to 30. As a result, page load times increased from 400 milliseconds to 900 milliseconds. This increase—just half a second—resulted in a 25% decrease in searches.

Google also experimented with adding a checkout icon to search results pages. This made pages roughly 2% slower—and led to a 2% reduction in searches per user.

## CASE STUDY: GQ CUTS LOAD TIME BY 80%, GROWS TRAFFIC BY 83%

In 2015, GQ found that its average load time had grown to a sluggish 7 seconds. The solution: a reboot that targeted ads and other third-party tags and features, as well as a migration to a single content management system. The newly stream-lined site reduced server calls by 400% and ultimately cut load times by 80%, down to just under 2 seconds.[14]

---

13 Dan Farber, "Google's Marissa Mayer: Speed wins," ZDNet, November 9, 2006.
14 Lucia Moses, "How GQ cut its webpage load time by 80 percent," Digiday, August 12, 2015.

The relaunched site quickly experienced a number of benefits, including:

- 83% traffic increase (from 6 million to 11 million unique visitors)
- 32% increase in time on site (from 5.9 minutes to 7.8 minutes)
- 108% increase in interaction rate with ads

## CASE STUDY: AT THE FINANCIAL TIMES, PAGE SLOWDOWNS CORRELATE TO UP TO 11% DECREASE IN ENGAGEMENT

*The Financial Times* wanted to understand how much the speed of its website affected two metrics:

- Session depth (also referred to as "conversion rate" within the study; this was defined as the number of articles read within a single user session)
- Revenue

They ran two consecutive tests, each roughly four weeks long.[15]

In the first test, subscribers were divided into two equal groups. The control group experienced the standard website. The other cohort experienced a 5-second delay to each page load (achieved by adding a blocking CSS call within the HTML).

The first test showed a significant drop in engagement from the slower group, so the test was repeated afterward. This time, users were segmented into four cohorts:

- The control group saw the website at normal speed (about 2 seconds).
- The second group saw a 1-second delay added to each page load.
- The third group saw a 2-second delay.
- The last group saw a 3-second delay.

In looking at the session depth metric, the team saw little impact for shorter visits (of two pages). But for users visiting three pages or more, they noted a grad-

---

15 Matt Chadburn and Gadi Lahav, "A Faster FT.com," Engine Room (Financial Times Technology Blog), April 4, 2016.

ual decline across all the test variants. The deeper the journey, the greater the drop-off in engagement.

At the slower speeds—5 seconds and 3 seconds—they saw this trend saturate around 10 pages (11% worse for 5 seconds, and 7.5% for the 3-seconds variant), but at 2 seconds and 1 second, the difference kept growing (see Figure 2-14).

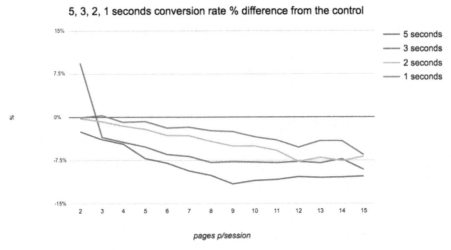

*Figure 2-14. FT.com found that page slowdowns resulted in decreased user engagement*

Not only did slower pages result in decreased user engagement within a single session, the study also found that the trend persisted—and even worsened—over time (Figure 2-15):

*Over the first seven days of a user arriving at the test and experiencing a one second delay we saw a 4.9% drop in the number of articles they read compared to the control group. The difference grew to 7.2% for the users in the three seconds delay variant.*

*After twenty-eight days of being in the test the difference grew for the two- and three-second variants, 4.4% to 5% and 7.2% to 7.9% respectively.*

*In conclusion, over the testing period users read fewer articles each day whilst experiencing delays loading each web page.*

| Page load time | 7 days impact | 28 days |
| --- | --- | --- |
| 1 second slower | -4.9% | -4.6% |
| 2 second slower | – | -5.0% |
| 3 second slower | -7.2% | -7.9% |

*Figure 2-15. Mean % drop in article views between variants and control*

## CASE STUDY: EDMUNDS.COM SHAVES 7 SECONDS OFF LOAD TIME, SEES 17% INCREASE IN PAGE VIEWS AND 3% INCREASE IN AD REVENUE

When Edmunds, a leading resource for car reviews, set out to redesign one of its web properties—InsideLine.com—the company wanted pages to load in less than 1.5 seconds. At the same time, they wanted to create richer content through the addition of photos, videos, and interactive components. Together, these would contribute to the greater goal of increasing revenue generated by ad impressions.

After trial and error, Edmunds was able to cut the home page load time from 9 seconds on the old site to 1.6 seconds on the redesigned site. The faster load time reduced impression discrepancies, ultimately increasing ad revenue by 3%. When these same principles were applied to their home page redesign, Edmunds enjoyed a 17% increase in page views per visit.[16]

## Customer Satisfaction and Retention

As every site owner knows, repeat customers are your bread and butter. Return visitors spend twice as much time on your site than first-time visitors. They also view more pages, and they're nine times more likely to make a purchase.

Getting a visitor to your site for the very first time isn't cheap. The average customer acquisition cost (CAC) for ecommerce sites can be anywhere between $75 and $120.

Turning your hard-won new visitors into repeat customers is difficult work. New customers can be fickle, and a slow online experience is one of the top

---

16 "How Edmunds Decreased Page Load Time by 80% in 3 Simple Steps," GoogleTechTalks (YouTube), January 13, 2011.

culprits in driving them away. As we've already covered earlier in this book, slow pages are one of the most common complaints—second only to security concerns—of online shoppers.

Poor web performance has a dramatic effect on customer satisfaction, both in terms of repeat visits and word of mouth. According to an Aberdeen survey of 116 companies,[17] a 1-second delay in load time equals, on average, a 16% decrease in customer satisfaction. Up to 49% of users who experience performance issues when completing a transaction will abandon the transaction and go to a competitor's site. Of these, 33% will never return to the site and 18% will share their experiences with others.

Page slowdowns affect your visitors who stick around, too. They may still use your business, but their overall usage is likely to decline—and that usage decline can persist even after you've made fixes to speed up your pages. Google found this out when they removed a 400-millisecond delay from their search results pages. Even when the pages returned to optimal performance, users still made 0.21% fewer searches.[18]

---

*First and foremost, we believe that speed is more than a feature.* **Speed is the most important feature.** *If your application is slow, people won't use it. I see this more with mainstream users than I do with power users. I think that power users sometimes have a bit of a sympathetic eye to the challenges of building really fast web apps, and maybe they're willing to live with it, but when I look at my wife and kids, they're my mainstream view of the world. If something is slow, they're just gone.*

**—FRED WILSON, VC, UNION SQUARE VENTURES (ETSY, TWITTER, TUMBLR, ZYNGA)**

---

17  "The Performance of Web Applications: Customers Are Won or Lost in One Second," Aberdeen Group, 2008.

18  Jake Brutlag, "Speed Matters," Google Research Blog, June 23, 2009.

**CASE STUDY: IMPACT OF PAGE SLOWDOWN ON RETURNING TRAFFIC**

In the page-slowdown experiment cited in "Page Views and Bounce Rate" on page 35, Strangeloop also monitored and analyzed user behavior for six weeks after the test ended, to gauge the long-term impact, if any, of slow performance, even after users began to receive accelerated pages.[19]

Even after the experiment was over and the shoppers in the 500-millisecond and 1000-millisecond delay groups were served the same optimized site as the baseline group, these individuals were significantly less likely to return to the site. Six weeks after the original test ended, return traffic began to slowly improve as visitors finally seemed to be recovering from their poor experience (Figure 2-16).

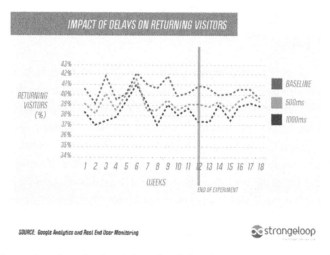

Figure 2-16. In an 18-week study, Strangeloop found that visitor return rates were affected even after page load times returned to normal

## Google Ranking and Organic Search Traffic

Google's goal is to offer a fast, streamlined experience to all Internet users. With performance affecting so many aspects of this experience, it's no surprise the company confirmed way back in 2010 that site speed is a factor in its search ranking algorithm—though the details are, understandably, a closely held secret.

---

19 Joshua Bixby, "Case study: The impact of HTML delay on mobile business metrics," Strangeloop Networks, 2011.

More recently, Google has taken a visible, aggressive tack in penalizing sites that perform poorly on mobile devices. In 2013, Google announced a plan to roll out several ranking changes that address sites that are misconfigured for smartphone users. The announcement mentioned two common mobile configuration mistakes that site owners should be mindful of:

*Faulty redirects*
> When a page redirects users to a generic mobile-optimized page, rather than a mobile-optimized version of the specific page they were searching for

*Smartphone-only errors*
> When mobile users are served an error page from search, instead of the page they were looking for

## The "Slow" Label

In early 2015, Google caused another stir when the company began experimenting with a "Slow" label in its mobile search results, warning users that some websites might be unacceptably slow on mobile devices (see Figure 2-17). The experiment (not surprisingly) caused a media stir, and Google (also not surprisingly) did not deign to comment on the specifics of this experiment.

But while Google's treatment of performance as a search ranking factor has attracted a fair bit of tech media attention and discussion over the past several years, I've never met a site owner who suddenly decided to prioritize performance because of it. This could be due to the fact that the details have always been murky, with most people agreeing that speed is probably just one relatively minor part of Google's search ranking algorithm. The "Slow" tag, however, may be too in your face to dismiss. It signals that Google is taking performance—and particularly mobile performance—increasingly seriously. Site owners would be wise to do the same.

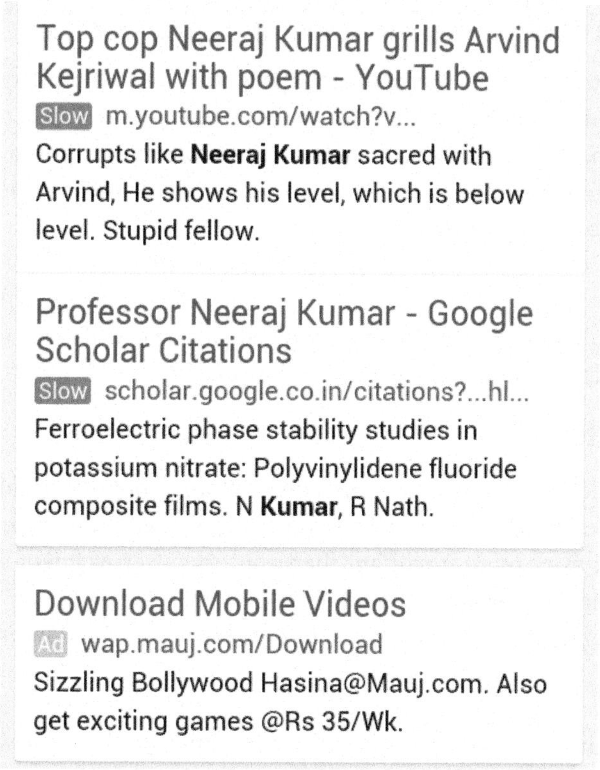

## Top cop Neeraj Kumar grills Arvind Kejriwal with poem - YouTube

`Slow` m.youtube.com/watch?v...

Corrupts like **Neeraj Kumar** sacred with Arvind, He shows his level, which is below level. Stupid fellow.

## Professor Neeraj Kumar - Google Scholar Citations

`Slow` scholar.google.co.in/citations?...hl...

Ferroelectric phase stability studies in potassium nitrate: Polyvinylidene fluoride composite films. N **Kumar**, R Nath.

## Download Mobile Videos

`Ad` wap.mauj.com/Download

Sizzling Bollywood Hasina@Mauj.com. Also get exciting games @Rs 35/Wk.

*Figure 2-17. Screen grab of Google's experimental "Slow" label from early 2015*

The impact of page speed on SEO can range from negligible to very noticeable, depending on the site. Speed may not be the most important ranking factor for search engines, but it is a factor nonetheless. As long as Google's search algorithm remains a mystery, site owners can't know what type of optimization improved their rank from page 3 to page 1. For some sites, faster pages could be that tipping point.

Regardless of how great or minor a ranking factor site speed is, you should care about how fast your pages are. SEO is just one benefit of serving faster pages. If you care about the entire end-to-end user experience—from your visitors being able to find your site quickly to being able to navigate and complete whatever tasks they need to complete—then you should care about page speed.

**CASE STUDY: SMARTFURNITURE.COM ACCELERATES PAGES, ENJOYS 20% INCREASE IN ORGANIC SEARCH TRAFFIC (PLUS MORE SALES!)**

Google's 2010 announcement that page speed was a search ranking factor solidified the notion of speed as a critical business issue for furnishings retailer Smartfurniture.com. The company's decision to optimize its site improved its search engine rankings by an average of two positions, and launched one search term from below 50th place up to third place.

These SEO improvements resulted in a 20% increase in organic traffic, a 14% increase in page views, and—most importantly—a significant sales bump. In addition to growing revenue, the improved page speed also led to greater customer satisfaction and increased average time on site.[20]

## Mobile Matters

Why do people abandon mobile transactions? It turns out that usability issues far outweigh other variables. Frustration over slow load times and complex payment processes are even more important than concerns over payment security when shoppers decide to give up a transaction.

According to a survey by Harris Interactive of the top concerns of mobile consumers:[21]

- One-third (32%) complain about mobile apps/sites being slow to load.
- 27% feel payment processes are too complicated.
- One in four (26%) cite difficulty with navigation.
- 16% reported concerns around security of payment info.

---

20  Margaret Kuchler, "The Growing Need For Speed: How Site Performance Increasingly Influences Search Rankings," Retail TouchPoints, May 19, 2011.

21  "Skava Consumer Mobile Shopping Survey," Harris Interactive (for Skava), 2013.

*As users migrate to mobile, page load time is perhaps the most important metric we have. If you can't load pages fast enough, you can't compete. Consumer expectations in a mobile-led world are extreme.*

**—HOWARD MITTMAN, VP AND PUBLISHER, GQ**

## CASE STUDY: MEASURING THE IMPACT OF PAGE SLOWDOWNS ON MOBILE METRICS

In 2011, Strangeloop conducted a split test[22] of a client's ecommerce site over the course of 12 weeks, in which mobile traffic was split into four groups: those who were served fully optimized pages, and those who were served pages that experienced artificially introduced HTML delays of 200, 500, and 1,000 milliseconds. The test monitored four metrics: bounce rate, conversion rate, cart size, and page views.

While the results of the 200-millisecond delay weren't significant, the 500-millisecond and 1,000-millisecond delays had a dramatic impact. Just a 1-second delay led to a 8.3% increase in bounce rate, a 3.5% decrease in conversion rate, a 2.1% hit to cart size, and a 9.4% loss in page views (see Figure 2-18).

|  | 200ms | 500ms | 1000ms |
|---|---|---|---|
| Bounce rate | --- | 4.7% | 8.3% |
| Conversion rate | --- | -1.9% | -3.5% |
| Cart size | --- | --- | -2.1% |
| Pageviews | -1.2% | -5.7% | -9.4% |

*Figure 2-18. Page load delays had a negative impact on bounce rate, conversion rate, cart size, and page views*

---

22 Joshua Bixby, "Case study: The impact of HTML delay on mobile business metrics," Strangeloop Networks, 2011.

As a follow-up to Strangeloop's study, four years later I studied the performance of another leading online retailer that enjoys a significant amount of mobile traffic. Looking at 4.5 million mobile user sessions, I correlated load time with conversion rate and bounce rate.

These were a few of the more compelling findings:

*In terms of conversions, the performance sweet spot was 2.4 seconds*

Pages that loaded in 2.4 seconds, on average, enjoyed the peak conversion rate (1.9%) during this 30-day span. Note that a 1.9% conversion rate for mobile is pretty respectable. This number approaches being commensurate with a typical desktop conversion rate of 2%–4%, which you usually see for retail sites.

*Pages that were just 1 second faster experienced a 27% conversion rate increase*

The conversion rate dropped to 1.5% for visitors who experience average page load times of 3.3 seconds. In other words, for this site, the conversion rate was 27% higher for visitors who enjoyed a load time that was about 1 second faster.

*At 4.2 seconds, the average conversion rate dropped below 1%*

Pages that were just 2 seconds slower experienced conversion rates that were cut by more than half. Or to put a more positive spin on this finding, pages that were just 2 seconds faster more than doubled their conversion rate

*By the 6-second mark, the conversion rate begins to plateau*

This is sometimes referred to as the "performance poverty line"—the point at which conversions more or less bottom out (see Figure 2-19).

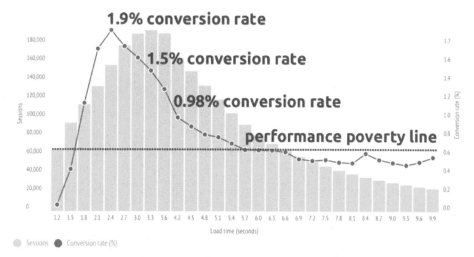

*Figure 2-19. In a study into retail mobile performance, the highest conversion rate was experienced by pages with an average load time of 2.4 seconds*

## Takeaway

In the last case study I cited, a 1-second improvement in median load time correlated to a 27% increase in conversion rate. Your mileage may vary depending on your business, your audience, your competitive context, and other usability factors on your site. The best way to understand how load time correlates to user/business metrics on your site is to look at your own user data.

The important thing to remember is that speed matters—even on mobile (and perhaps especially on mobile). Even if pages are already relatively fast, optimizing them further can pay off.

# 3

# Measuring Performance from Within

So far, we've focused on the monetary benefits of improving web performance for customers. In this chapter, let's switch gears and discuss the value of performance optimization using inward-facing metrics.

A 2008 study by researchers at Aberdeen Group[1] found that application performance issues could hurt overall corporate revenues by up to 9%. These findings don't just apply to KPIs such as conversions and revenues. Poor application performance can hurt companies in a myriad of other ways, including:

- Collaboration and information sharing

- Task completion

- Customer service (order management, customer records, problem resolution, call center efficiency, etc.)

- Adoption rate for internal applications

- Datacenter infrastructure costs

- Bandwidth costs

---

1 "The Performance of Web Applications: Customers Are Won or Lost in One Second," Aberdeen Group, 2008.

In this chapter, we'll discuss each of these alongside real-world stories that show how companies correlated performance improvements to internal metrics.

---

*I really believe that if we're to going to continue to recruit people to contribute to the pages, it really needs to give people that user experience. It needs to not just be fast, but delightfully fast.*

**—ORI LIVNEH, PRINCIPAL SOFTWARE ENGINEER,**
**WIKIMEDIA FOUNDATION**

---

## Employee Satisfaction

*[Frontend optimization] significantly improves the speed of our application, which not only increases employee productivity, but does wonders for our bottom line.*

**—ALAN RUTH, SENIOR DIRECTOR, ENTERPRISE APPLICATIONS, GRAEBEL**

Have you ever wondered how much time people in your company spend waiting for internal apps to load?

Graebel, a global provider of employee and commercial relocation services, asked this question within their own company, and the results were surprising. They calculated that, in just one small department of 20 people, those people spent a total of 130 hours per month—in other words, almost an entire month's worth of work hours for one person—waiting for the pages of a single internal web-based application to load.[2]

Employees could aptly be described as the "internal customers" of your business. If they're waiting more than 2 seconds for internal applications to respond, it's hurting your bottom line. Going back as far as 1982, research conducted by IBM[3] made a strong connection between application response time and worker productivity. In one study, the number of tasks that a department was able to

---

2 "For Graebel, a Faster Web Application Equals Happier, More Productive Employees," Radware, 2013.

3 Ben Shneiderman, "Response Time and Display Rate in Human Performance with Computers," Computing Surveys, Vol.16, No.3, September 1984.

complete in an hour more than doubled when application performance improved by just 2.7 seconds.

IBM also found that not only does latency affect the number of tasks an employee can perform, but "as the application becomes more responsive, the employee becomes exponentially more productive."

Remember usability expert Jakob Nielsen's findings about response time and human behavior: 10 seconds is about the limit for keeping a user's attention focused on a nonresponsive dialogue. After 10 seconds, even the most efficient worker has to struggle to refocus on the task at hand.

## Slow Performance Hurts Morale

As we covered back in Chapter 1, repeated interruptions—including, but not limited to, page load delays—are a huge detriment to concentration, and by extension, productivity. Beyond productivity losses, poor performance also affects morale. Not only do small delays add up quickly, but users—both internal and external—must concentrate up to 50% harder when pages or applications are slow. And while most of us are fairly good at developing short-term strategies that let us deal with repeated interruptions, this often comes at the expense of our overall satisfaction and our willingness to take on new tasks.

As study after study has proven, human beings are really good at convincing ourselves that we understand what makes us happy, and we're really bad at actually knowing what makes us happy. Because of this, it's easy to fool ourselves into believing that because our productivity is more or less the same—and because we place a great deal of value on productivity—somehow this equates to happiness.

In other words, we can convince ourselves that we're fine—or if you're an employer, you can convince yourself that your workers are fine—when perhaps we're not.

## Consumer Web Applications Have Raised the Bar for Performance

Employee expectations of performance, reliability, and usability have been set by the consumer web applications we use every day. We humans aren't good at compartmentalizing our demands. Because Twitter, Pinterest, and Facebook are fast, we expect our other tools and systems—from CRM to MIS—to be equally fast.

Enterprise IT has to meet those expectations. Without a watchful eye on user experience, multimillion dollar IT initiatives can go to waste as workers give up on slow, hard-to-use new tools and revert to old, familiar, more costly ways of doing their jobs.

To summarize, improved application performance helps employee productivity by:

- Increasing the number of web-based tasks employees can complete in a given time frame
- Reducing web stress and frustration
- Improving employee satisfaction and confidence
- Increasing the adoption rate of internal applications

Keeping users happy is one of the human-facing benefits of making apps and websites responsive. In an ideal world, that should be enough reason to commit to performance, but if that isn't quite a compelling enough argument for you, there's a potentially huge technological benefit, too, which I'll cover in the next section.

## Bandwidth

"Bandwidth doesn't matter."

It's hard to believe, but this idea is still bandied about in the web design and development community (though hopefully less often than it used to be). With the advent of faster networks, many people naively believe that bandwidth concerns are no longer relevant. That's partly because promises of ever-greater bandwidth are good PR for telecom providers. The public and the media latch on to these promises because they sound great. "Double the bandwidth" sounds fantastic if you believe that "double the bandwidth" means "twice as fast." (It doesn't. In fact, increasing bandwidth by 1,000% improves page load times by only about 50%—but this isn't something you'll ever hear from a service provider. I'll elaborate on this in the next chapter.)

Page speed aside, any mobile user who is sensitive to their data cap—and to those monthly bills from their telecom provider—will tell you that, for them, bandwidth truly does still matter.

Being dinged for an extra $20 every so often from your mobile service provider is annoying and unwelcome, but this is a drop in the bucket compared to the massive costs that business owners accrue when they send data-heavy pages over the wire. Bandwidth is a costly commodity. For high-traffic websites, bandwidth is probably responsible for the majority of your IT spend—easily surpassing hosting and storage costs.

## Page Bloat (or, When Can We Expect the Average Web Page to Hit 3 MB?)

Bloated pages are widely recognized bandwidth hogs, yet pages keep getting fatter. In 2015, the average web page weighed in at over 2 MB in size (according to the HTTP Archive, which gathers page data for roughly the top half million websites worldwide). This is up from 1 MB just three years earlier. Back in 2012, many people were shocked to learn that the average page was 1 MB in size. It's amazing how quickly we grow accustomed to findings like this.

It's important to remember that these numbers are just averages. While many pages are smaller than 2 MB, it's also not uncommon to encounter pages that exceed 5 or even 10 MB.

At this rate of growth, could the average page hit 3 MB by 2017? Only time will tell, but one thing is certain: page growth is inevitable (see Figure 3-1).

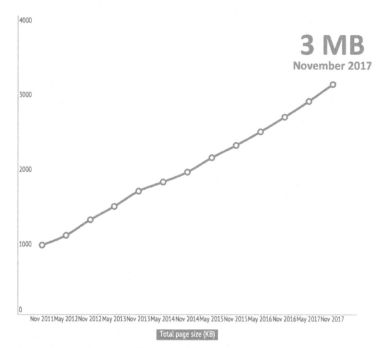

*Figure 3-1. Plotting the trajectory of page growth using HTTP Archive data, it's possible that the average page could reach 3 MB by the end of 2017*

There are a lot of ingredients in today's web pages—scripts, stylesheets, videos, custom fonts—and these ingredients are all factors behind the growing obesity of the modern Web. But the biggest ingredient is images, which account for more than 60% of the average page's total weight (on an image-rich site, this number can creep up to 85%!).

## CASE STUDY: WIKIPEDIA IMPROVES LOAD TIMES BY 66%, RADICALLY CUTS BACK ON NEW SERVER COSTS

It's somewhat ironic that "wiki" is a Hawaiian word for "quick," and yet the Wikimedia Foundation found themselves with a site that had bogged down to the point that the median page-saving time for wiki editors was 7.5 seconds.

As anyone who's spent time using Wikipedia knows, editors are the site's lifeblood. They're the chief contributors and curators of content. While the bulk of Wikipedia users are served pages relatively quickly from CDN PoPs, this isn't the case for editors, who for obvious reasons need real-time access to pages. For these editors, the user experience hinges directly on the performance of the MediaWiki app servers. Yet unlike the vast majority of visitors who experience a fast, cached version of the site, editors experienced a gradual slowdown in Wikipedia's performance.

To address this issue, the Wikimedia Foundation deployed a new technology called HipHop Virtual Machine, or HHVM, which sped up MediaWiki, Wikipedia's underlying PHP-based code. HHVM reduced the median page-saving time for editors from about 7.5 seconds to 2.5 seconds (Figures 3-2, 3-3, and 3-4).

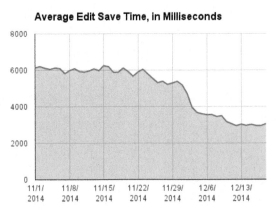

Figure 3-2. Wikipedia reduced the median page-saving time for editors from 7.5 seconds to 2.5 seconds

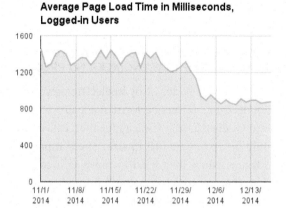

*Figure 3-3. Wikipedia cut average page loads from around 1.3 seconds to under 1 second*

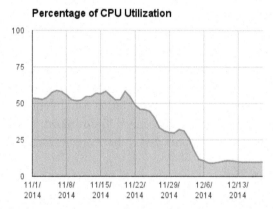

*Figure 3-4. As a result of optimizations, CPU load on Wikipedia servers decreased from 50% to 10%*

As a result of deploying HHVM, Wikipedia experienced performance gains[4] across a number of user experience and backend metrics, such as:

- Average page load time for logged-in users dropped by about 30%, from 1.3 seconds to 0.9 seconds.
- CPU load on app servers decreased from around 50% to 10%.

---

4 Ori Livneh, "How we made editing Wikipedia twice as fast," Wikimedia Blog, December 29, 2014.

- Drastically cut plans to purchase new app servers.

## CASE STUDY: HYDRO-QUÉBEC REDUCED DOWNLOAD TIMES BY 90%, INCREASED ADOPTION RATE OF NEW ENGINEERING PROCESSES

Hydro-Québec, the primary provider of hydroelectric power in Québec, Canada, had been experiencing some serious performance pains with a CAD app shared over its WAN. Hydro-Québec used a CAD application called CATIA to create digital models that could be up to 600 MB in size. The company ran into extremely slow performance issues when they tried to move to a concurrent engineering process, which relies on employees having nigh-immediate access to shared files.

"Response time was ugly," according to Daniel Brisebois, Hydro-Québec's IT advisor. In one stopwatch test, the company found that even a relatively small 14 MB CATIA file took 15 minutes to download over a typical 10 Mbps connection with 15 milliseconds latency. In addition, people in remote offices couldn't even work with CATIA without 30- to 60-second delays between every mouse click.

One of the main benefits of concurrent engineering is real-time collaboration, but with these performance issues, collaboration was next to impossible.

After optimizing its WAN, Hydro-Québec reported benefits[5] such as fewer errors, a faster engineering cycle, and enhanced data integrity. As a for instance, a 17 MB file that formerly took 85 seconds to download took just 8 seconds to download after the WAN was optimized. Other benefits included:

- CATIA file download time reduced by almost 90%
- Increased adoption rate of concurrent engineering processes
- Reduction in procedural errors
- Fewer engineering problems due to document mismatches
- Fewer errors caused by working with outdated files
- Faster engineering cycles
- Enhanced data integrity
- Office applications ran 10 to 25 times faster
- Reduced network data by 90%

---

5 "Concurrent Engineering Is Possible over a WAN," Riverbed Case Study, 2011.

In terms of cost savings, WAN optimization allowed Hydro-Québec to implement concurrent engineering for about 50% less than it would have cost if they had gone with another approach, such as buying dedicated servers and more software licenses. The company also estimates that through consolidation (maintaining only a single server in the home office), Hydro-Québec has saved as much as $1.5 million in avoided IT costs.

### CASE STUDY: NETFLIX SAW A 43% DECREASE IN ITS BANDWIDTH BILL AFTER ONE SIMPLE OPTIMIZATION

If you're trying to make your pages faster, your goal should be to make them lighter and leaner. That means eliminating unnecessary page assets, and then ensuring that those that remain are as small as they can be. This not only makes your pages load faster, but it also helps you save on your bandwidth bill.

One of the easiest and most effective optimizations is gzipping your plain text components. This doesn't cost any developer time, as all it involves is simply flipping a switch in your server configuration.

When Bill Scott, former head of UIE at Netflix, started at work at the video delivery giant, he noticed that gzip was not enabled. So he had it turned on.[6] As illustrated in Figure 3-5, the results were a huge immediate reduction in outbound network traffic.

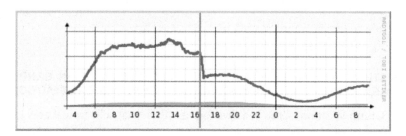

*Figure 3-5. Netflix gzip*

This network traffic reduction had several benefits, including:

- Payload reduced in some cases 15x (typically in half)
- 13%–25% improvement to user experience performance

---

6 Bill Scott, "Improving Netflix Performance," June 23, 2008.

- Bandwidth savings of 43%

## CASE STUDY: SHOPZILLA DECREASED LOAD TIMES BY 5 SECONDS, REDUCED INFRASTRUCTURE BY 50%

Shopzilla (now Connexity) is a leading shopping comparison service that became the poster child for web performance optimization when it shared a powerful case study back in 2009.

The site had accumulated years of technical debt as the company's family of sites became increasingly monolithic. The company took what was, at the time, a huge gamble in radically re-architecting its entire online operation with an eye toward reducing infrastructure and improving performance.

After a 16-month re-engineering initiative, Shopzilla sped up its average page load time from 6 seconds to 1.2 seconds and experienced benefits[7] across a swath of business metrics:

- 7%–12% increase in conversion rate
- 5%–12% increase in top-line revenue (due to both intra-session performance drivers and an overall increase in sessions driven by search engine traffic)
- 25% increase in page views
- 50% reduction in infrastructure

## CASE STUDY: HILTON SPEEDS INTERNAL APP, RESULTING IN BANDWIDTH SAVINGS, GREATER CUSTOMER MORALE, AND EMPLOYEE SATISFACTION

Hilton Grand Vacations Club is a division of Hilton that sells timeshares to international customers. The company was experiencing major latency issues that caused delays of up to 30 minutes for a vital contract-processing app.

Hilton's senior director of technology applications, Rich Jackson, said that:

*Getting contracts approved is a time-consuming process that involves pushing large amounts of data to our central office in Orlando. In Asia, the contract process is more complex and requires more bandwidth than it does in the United States. Since it wasn't possible to duplicate our main*

---

7 Phil Dixon, "Shopzilla Site Redesign: We get what we measure," 2009.

*business systems and processes in our Japanese offices, it was taking up to 30 minutes to complete the IT portion of the contracts process...*

*As you can imagine, with the customer is sitting in front of you while you are waiting on a computer process, it's not an ideal situation. When you're processing a contract, time is of the essence. You don't want delays due to technology issues.*

Hilton implemented WAN optimization technology that accelerated this contract-processing app. After accelerating the app, the contract process was reduced from more than 30 minutes to just a minute or two. Benefits of this optimization included:

- Data reduction capabilities reduced the company's bandwidth utilization by up to 80% (these cost savings are felt particularly in Japan, where bandwidth is at a premium).
- "The time spent waiting for contracts to process has been greatly improved, which has had a huge effect on customer and employee satisfaction."

## Takeaway

If you only take one thing away from reading this chapter, I hope it's this: not only does performance affect both hard (technology) and soft (people) metrics, these metrics are inextricably interconnected. Almost any change to your technology stack affects the people who engage with that stack.

Or put it this way: it doesn't matter if you're a hard-hearted Scrooge McDuck type who cares only about cutting infrastructure and bandwidth costs. If you tackle performance with those objectives in mind, you're inevitably going to make your users measurably happier. (Sorry, Uncle Scrooge!)

# 4

# Let's Talk Solutions

Concerns about web performance aren't new. Let's jump into the Wayback Machine and make a quick visit to 1999, when Zona released a report[1] warning online retailers that they risked losing $4.35 billion per year if they didn't optimize their websites' loading times. (Interesting aside: Zona recommended that the optimal loading time for ecommerce sites was 8 seconds. Times sure have changed. Today, we know that for most ecommerce sites, the performance sweet spot is around 2.5 seconds. After 4 seconds, conversion rates dip sharply.)

Over the years, solutions have become increasingly refined, from building out the bulk of the infrastructure of the Internet to homing in on performance issues within the browser. This chapter offers a quick fly-over tour—designed expressly for nongeeks—of the acceleration and optimization landscape over the past 20 or so years.

The goal here is to show you how solutions have evolved from relatively simple (i.e., throw more servers at the problem) to increasingly complex and nuanced as we've learned more about the root causes of performance issues and how to address them.

Before getting started with talking about solutions, let's first talk about two of the biggest problems faced by anyone who cares about making the Internet faster:

- Network latency (AKA the amount of time it takes for a packet of data to get from one point to another)

---

1 "The Economic Impacts of Unacceptable Web-Site Download Speeds," Zona Research, April 1999.

- The myth that modern networks are so fast, we no longer need to worry about latency

## What Is Latency—And Why Should You Care About It?

Before we start talking about solutions, it's helpful to identify some of the main problems. If you ask anyone in the performance industry to name the biggest obstacles to delivering faster user experiences, "latency" would probably be one of their top three answers.

Here's a (very high-level) layperson-friendly definition of latency: as a web user, as soon as you visit a page, your browser sends out requests to all the servers that host the resources (images, JavaScript files, third-party content, etc.) that make up that page. Latency is the time it takes for those resources to travel through the Internet "pipe" and get to your browser.

Let's put this in real-world terms. Say you visit a web page and that page contains 100 resources. Your browser has to make 100 individual requests to the site's host server (or more likely, multiple servers) in order to pull those objects. Each of those requests experiences 75–140 milliseconds of latency. This may not sound like much, but it adds up fast. When you consider that a page can easily contain 300 or more resources, and that latency can reach a full *second* for some mobile users, you can see where latency becomes a major performance problem.

One of the big problems with latency is that it's unpredictable and inconsistent. It can be affected by factors ranging from the weather to what your neighbors are downloading.

Tackling latency is a top priority for the performance industry. There are several ways to do this:

- Shorten the server round-trips by bringing content closer to users.
- Reduce the total number of round-trips.
- Allow more browser-to-server requests to happen concurrently.
- Improve the browser cache, so that it can (a) store files and serve them where relevant on subsequent pages in a visit, and (b) store and serve files for repeat visits.

While latency isn't the only performance challenge, it's a major one. Throughout the rest of this chapter, I'll explain how various performance-boosting technologies address latency (and other issues).

## Network Infrastructure (or, Why More Bandwidth Isn't Enough)

A conversation about performance-enhancing technologies couldn't take place without first acknowledging the huge advances made to the backbone of the Internet itself.

We've come a long way since 1993, when the World Wide Web was introduced. Back then, we were too busy being excited and amazed about the simple fact that the Internet existed to complain about the slowness of the network. Not that faster networks would have made much of a difference to how we experienced the Web. For most of us, dial-up Internet access was limited to 56 Kbps modems connecting via phone lines.

Not surprisingly, even the minimalist web pages of those times—when the average page was around 14 KB in size and contained just two resources—could take a while to load. (True story: I have a friend who taught herself to play the guitar while waiting for pages to load in her early months of using the Web.)

Today, you'd be forgiven for believing that, between our faster networks and superior connectivity, we've fully mitigated our early performance problems—and not a moment too soon. Modern web pages can easily reach 3 or 4 MB in size. When I hear people rationalize why this kind of page bloat isn't a serious performance issue, one of the most common arguments that comes up is the belief that our ever-evolving networks mitigate the impact.

### DO NETWORK IMPROVEMENTS ACTUALLY MAKE WEB PAGES LOAD MORE QUICKLY?

While yes, it's true that networks and connectivity have improved, there are some misconceptions about what those improvements mean in real-world usage. To illustrate, let's consider the results of a set of performance tests of the Etsy.com home page, using WebPagetest.org, a synthetic performance measurement tool that simulates different realistic connection speeds and latencies. (If you want to jump straight to the key findings, skip ahead to the end of this section.)

The page was tested across five different desktop and mobile connection types (RTT stands for round-trip time—that is, the amount of time it takes for the host server to receive, process, and deliver on a request for a page resource such as images, CSS files, and so on; "latency" is another word for the delay in RTT):

- FIOS (20/5 Mbps, 4ms RTT)
- Cable (5/1 Mbps, 28ms RTT)
- DSL (1.5 Mbps/384 Kbps, 50ms RTT)
- Mobile 3G – Fast (1.6 Mbps/768 Kbps, 150ms RTT)
- Mobile 3G – Slow (780/330 Kbps, 200ms RTT)

Taking a glance at Figure 4-1, you can see that the light blue bars representing load times are not nearly as dramatically stacked as the darker blue bars that indicate bandwidth numbers.

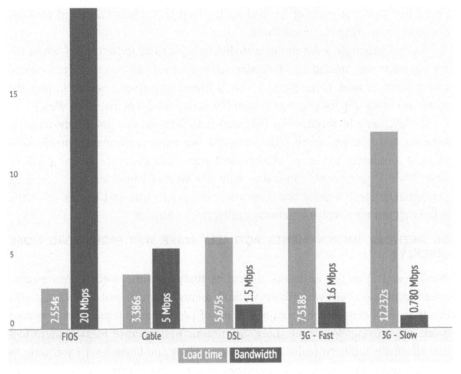

*Figure 4-1. Median load times for the Etsy.com home page across a variety of different connections (via WebPagetest.com, a synthetic performance measurement tool)*

Figure 4-2 is another way of looking at these numbers. If people's supposition that bandwidth improvements correlate to proportionately faster load times was correct, then the two sides of this second graph would mirror each other. Clearly they do not.

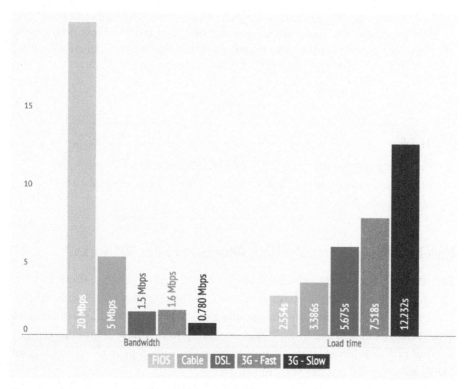

*Figure 4-2. Another way of looking at Etsy.com's performance results across connection types; if bandwidth increases correlated to proportionately faster load times, then this pair of graphs would mirror each other*

A few observations:

- While download bandwidth is 300% greater for FIOS (20 Mbps) than it is for cable (5 Mbps), the median load time over FIOS (2.554 seconds) is only 24.6% faster than the median load time over cable (3.386 seconds).

- The distinction becomes even more pronounced when you compare DSL to FIOS. Bandwidth is 1,233% greater for FIOS than it is for DSL (20 Mbps versus 1.5 Mbps), yet median load time over FIOS is only 55% faster than over DSL (2.554 seconds versus 5.675 seconds).

- While DSL and "3G – Fast" have comparable bandwidth (1.5 Mbps versus 1.6 Mbps), the 3G connection is 32.5% slower (5.675 seconds versus 7.518

seconds). The key differentiator between these two connections isn't bandwidth—it's latency. The 3G connection has a RTT of 150ms, compared to the DSL RTT of 50ms.

- You can see the combined impact of latency and bandwidth when you compare the fast and slow 3G connections. The fast connection has 105% greater bandwidth than the slow connection, yet the median page load is only 38.5% faster (7.518 seconds versus 12.232 seconds).

---

**TL;DR**

Increasing bandwidth by up to 1,233% resulted in pages that were just 55% faster—meaning that faster networks aren't the performance cureall that some folks assume they are.

---

## How Many People Actually Have Access to Faster Networks?

Even if modern networks fully delivered the speed that we'd like to think they do, it's important to know that a large proportion of Internet users can't access them.

In 2015, the Federal Communications Commission updated its definition of broadband from 4 Mbps to 25 Mbps. According to this new definition, roughly one out of five Internet users—approximately 50 million people—in the United States suddenly did not have broadband access.

Some of the FCC's other findings[2] included (Figure 4-3):

- More than half of all rural Americans lack broadband access, and 20% lack access even to 4 Mbps service.

- 63% of residents on tribal lands and in US territories lack broadband access.

- 35% of US schools lack access to "fiber networks capable of delivering the advanced broadband required to support today's digital-learning tools."

- Overall, the broadband availability gap closed by only 3% between 2014 and 2015.

---

2 "FCC Finds U.S. Broadband Deployment Not Keeping Pace," Federal Communications Commission, February 4, 2015.

- When broadband is available, Americans living in urban and rural areas adopt it at very similar rates.

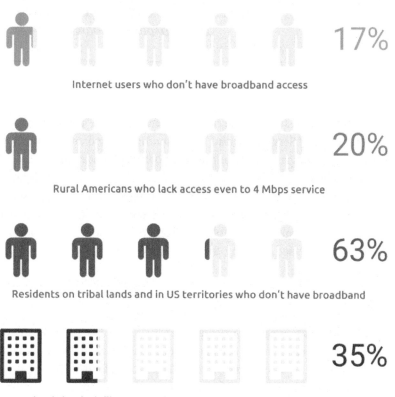

17%

Internet users who don't have broadband access

20%

Rural Americans who lack access even to 4 Mbps service

63%

Residents on tribal lands and in US territories who don't have broadband

35%

School that lack fiber networks necessary to support digital learning

FCC, 2015 Broadband Progress Report

*Figure 4-3. According to the FCC, a sizeable portion of people living in the United States lack anything remotely resembling high-speed Internet service*

Whether you're a site owner, developer, designer, or any other member of the Internet-using population, chances are you fall into the general category of urban broadband user. And there's also a chance that you believe your own speedy user experience is typical of all users. This isn't the case.

---

*We invented the Internet. We can do audacious things if we set big goals, and I think our new threshold, frankly, should be 100 Mbps. I think anything short of that shortchanges our children, our future, and our new digital economy.*

**—JESSICA ROSENWORCEL, FCC COMMISSIONER,**
***2015 BROADBAND PROGRESS REPORT***

---

## Servers

For much of the history of the Internet, performance problems have been blamed on servers. "Server overload" was commonly cited as the culprit behind everything from sluggish response times to poor page rendering. So the catch-all cure for performance pains emerged: throw more servers at the problem.

The myth that server load was the cause of most performance issues began to be put to rest in 2007, when Steve Souders's book *High Performance Web Sites* (O'Reilly)—which remains the bible for frontend developers and performance engineers—was released. In 2007, Steve famously said:

*80%–90% of the end user response time is spent on the frontend. Start there.*

This finding has proven consistent over the years. For the majority of sites, only 10%–20% of response time happens at the backend. To illustrate, Figure 4-4 shows the proportion of backend time (in blue) compared to frontend time (in green). In this specific instance, 86% of response time happened at the frontend.

The takeaway from this: yes, you do need to ensure that your servers are up to the task of hosting your site and meeting traffic demands, but chances are you're already covered in this area.

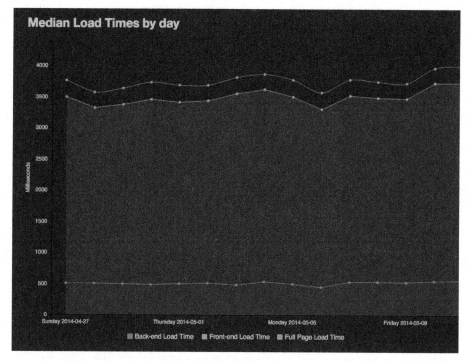

*Figure 4-4. Frontend (green) versus backend (blue) load times for a leading ecommerce site*

## Load Balancers and ADCs

A major advance occurred in the late 1990s, when server engineers recognized that, just as routing enabled more wires to carry more messages, load balancing could enable more servers to handle more requests. Individual web servers gave way to server farms and datacenters. These server farms equipped themselves with load balancers—technology that (as its name suggests) balances traffic load across multiple servers, preventing overload caused by traffic surges.

By 2007, load balancers had evolved into sophisticated application delivery controllers (ADCs). I should mention here that the issue of whether ADCs evolved from load balancers is the subject of some hairsplitting, with many folks arguing that ADCs are much more than just advanced load balancers. But for our purposes here, it's sufficient to know that the two technologies are frequently connected, even if they're evolutionarily light years apart.

In addition to simple load balancing, modern ADCs optimize database queries, helping speed up the dynamic construction of pages using stored data. ADCs also monitor server health, implement advanced routing strategies, and offload server tasks such as SSL termination and TCP connection management.

## Content Delivery Networks (CDNs)

As websites continued to compete for attention, page content shifted from being mostly styled text to containing a huge variety of images and other media. Support for stylesheets and client-side scripts further added to the number of objects that browsers needed to fetch in order to render each page. This multiplying of requests per page also multiplied the impact of network latency, which led to the next big innovation: content delivery networks.

While CDNs also solve performance-related problems such as improving global availability and reducing bandwidth, the main problem they address is latency: the amount of time it takes for the host server to receive, process, and deliver on a request for a page resource (images, CSS files, etc.). Latency depends largely on how far away the user is from the server, and it's compounded by the number of resources a web page contains.

For example, if all your resources are hosted in a server farm somewhere in Iowa, and a user is coming to your page from Berlin, then each request has to make a long round-trip from Berlin to Iowa and back to Berlin. If your web page contains 100 resources (which is at the low end of normal), then your visitor's browser has to make 100 individual requests to your server in order to retrieve those objects.

A CDN caches static resources in distributed servers (AKA edge caches, points of presence, or PoPs) throughout a region or worldwide, thereby bringing resources closer to users and reducing round-trip time (Figure 4-5).

Like any technology, CDNs have evolved over the years. First-generation CDNs, which were introduced in the late 1990s, focused simply on caching page resources. More recent iterations allow you to cache dynamic content and even develop on the edge.

While using a CDN is a must for many sites, it's not necessary for every site. For example, if you're hosting locally and if your users are also primarily local, a CDN won't make you much faster (though it can still help lighten your bandwidth bill).

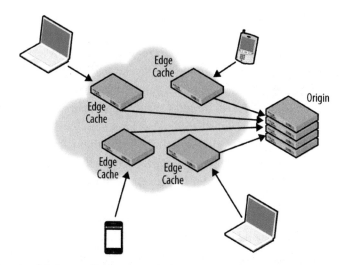

*Figure 4-5. A simplified view of how a CDN deploys edge caches, bringing static page assets closer to end users*

A CDN is not a standalone performance solution. There are a number of performance pains a CDN can't cure, such as:

- Server-side processing
- Third-party scripts that block the rest of the page from rendering
- Badly optimized pages, in which nonessential content renders before primary content
- Unoptimized images (e.g., images that are uncompressed, unconsolidated, nonprogressive, and/or in the wrong format)
- Unminified code

Your CDN can't help you with any of those problems. This is where frontend optimization comes in.

## Frontend Optimization (FEO)

Building out high-speed networks, load balancing within the datacenter, reducing network latency with CDNs—these are all effective performance solutions, but they're not enough.

CDNs address the performance middle mile by bringing resources closer to users—shortening server round-trips, and as a result, making pages load faster.

Frontend optimization (FEO) tackles performance at the frontend so that pages render more efficiently in the browser.

Frontend optimization addresses performance at the browser level, and has emerged in recent years as an extremely effective way to supplement server build-out and CDN services. One way that FEO alleviates latency is by consolidating page objects into bundles. Fewer bundles means fewer trips to the server, so the total latency hit is greatly reduced. FEO also leverages the browser cache and allows it to do a better job of storing files and serving them again where relevant, so that the browser doesn't have to make repeat calls to the server.

The four main FEO strategies for improving performance are:

- Reduce the number of HTTP requests required to fetch the resources for each page (by consolidating resources).

- Reduce the size of the payload needed to fulfill each request (by compressing resources).

- Optimize client-side processing priorities and improve script execution efficiency (by ensuring that critical page resources load first, and deferring noncritical resources).

- Target the specific capabilities of the client browser making each request (such as by leveraging the unique caching capabilities of each browser).

All of these strategies require changes to the HTML of the web page and changes to the objects being fetched by the page.

Steve Souders brought attention to frontend optimization with his book *High Performance Web Sites*. At the time, the only way to optimize your pages was by hand, via highly talented developers. Over the years, FEO has evolved into a highly sophisticated set of practices, some of which can only be performed by hardware- or software-based solutions.

While frontend optimization can be performed manually by developers, many site owners have turned to products and services that automate the process of page optimization. These tools implement FEO best practices by automatically modifying HTML in real time as pages are being served. Some CDNs now offer FEO as a value-added service.

### Auto-Preloading: Anatomy of an Advanced FEO Best Practice

Auto-preloading (not to be confused with browser preloading) is a sophisticated FEO technique. While browser preloading is initiated by the browser and focuses solely on the current page, auto-preloading happens near the origin and focuses on subsequent pages in a user's path through a website or application.

While browser preloading delivers up to 20% improvement, according to Mozilla and Google, auto-preloading can deliver up to 70% acceleration gain.

Auto-preloading takes advantage of two things:

- The advent of highly intelligent, dynamic analytics engines
- The amount of time a user spends viewing a page

The analytics engine observes and records every user path made by every single user who visits a website. This generates a massive amount of user data. Based on this massive amount of data, the engine can predict with a high degree of accuracy where a user is likely to go based on the page they're currently on and the previous pages they've visited. The solution then quietly preloads the resources for those "next" pages in the visitor's browser cache, so they're waiting on standby.

When you consider the fact that a typical web page can contain dozens of images alone, and that images comprise about half a page's weight, it's easy to see how auto-preloading images into the browser cache can deliver significant performance gains. It's an excellent workaround for the latency problem, which is arguably the number-one enemy of performance.

## Mobile Optimization

Today, roughly one out of four people worldwide own a smartphone. By 2020, that number is expected to increase to four out of five (see Figure 4-6). That's more than six billion mobile devices all connected to this massive infrastructure. Stop and think about that for a minute.

By 2020, 4 out of 5 people worldwide
will own a smartphone

*Figure 4-6. Ericsson, 2015 Mobility Report*

With the proliferation of mobile devices has come a host of unique issues that deeply affect mobile performance, from low-horsepower devices to network slowdowns.

One of the biggest performance issues (and one that is not unique to mobile) is page bloat. Pages served to mobile continue to balloon beyond our networks' ability to serve them (see Figure 4-7).

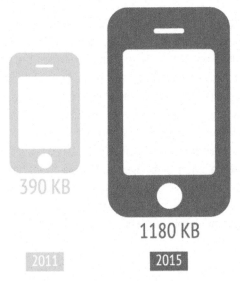

*Figure 4-7. According to the HTTP Archive, the average page served to a mobile device is well over 1 MB in size—three times larger than it was in 2011*

Despite these constraints, user expectations continue to grow: a typical mobile user expects a site to load as fast—or faster!—on their tablet or smartphone as it does on desktop.

Developing mobile-specific optimization techniques is the newest FEO frontier. These are just a few of the issues and opportunities mobile FEO seeks to address:

- Mobile networks are usually slower than those available to desktop machines, so reducing requests and payloads takes on added importance.
- Mobile browsers are slower to parse HTML and slower to execute JavaScript, so optimizing client-side processing is crucial.
- Mobile browser caches are much smaller than those of desktop browsers, requiring new approaches to leveraging local storage of resources that are reused on multiple pages of a user session.
- Small-screen mobile devices present opportunities for speeding transmission and rendering by resizing images so as not to waste bandwidth, processing time, and cache space.

Our use of mobile devices is exploding. Our expectations for performance are unrelenting. And modern websites place ever-increasing levels of strain on mobile networks, devices, and browsers. Mobile is arguably the greatest battlefield for performance today.

## Performance Measurement

Getting an accurate measurement for how long it took a web page to load used to be difficult and somewhat imperfect. In the olden days (you know, 2005), if you built a website, you had zero ability to look outside your own datacenters to get an understanding of performance. As websites evolved, the digital experiences we were able to serve over the Web became more and more complex. Images, video, and other rich content added more and more delay, which ultimately hurt the user's experience.

Unfortunately, in the past, none of this could be captured with simple backend measurements. This lack of visibility into the user experience drove website owners to look at different ways of measuring performance. This yielded advanced measurement capabilities like synthetic measurement and, later, real user monitoring. Finally, with these tools, site owners could see beyond the walls of their organization to get a real sense of how their applications were performing in the wild.

Website monitoring solutions fall into two types: synthetic and real user monitoring (RUM). Each of these types offers invaluable insight into how your site performs, but neither one is a standalone. Rather, they're highly complementary and can be used to gain a 360-degree view of performance.

## SYNTHETIC PERFORMANCE MEASUREMENT

Synthetic performance measurement (which you may sometimes hear called "active monitoring") is a simulated health check of your site. You create scripts that simulate an action or path that an end user would take on your site, and those paths are monitored at set intervals.

### What synthetic performance testing can tell you

Synthetic performance tests offer a unique set of capabilities that complement RUM extremely well. In addition to offering page-level diagnostics, synthetic tools allow you to measure a number of metrics—such as response time, load time, number of page assets, and page size—from a variety of different connection types. You can also test your site in production to find problems before the site goes live.

These are just a few of the questions that synthetic measurement can answer for you:

*How do you compare to your competitors?*
> Unlike real user monitoring, synthetic tools let you test any site on the Web, not just your own (Figure 4-8).

*How does the design of your pages affect performance?*
> Synthetic measurement gives you an object-level detail of page assets, letting you closely inspect the design and physical make-up of a page in a controlled environment.

*How does the newest version of your site compare to previous versions?*
> Benchmark performance before and after new deployments in order to pinpoint what made pages faster or slower.

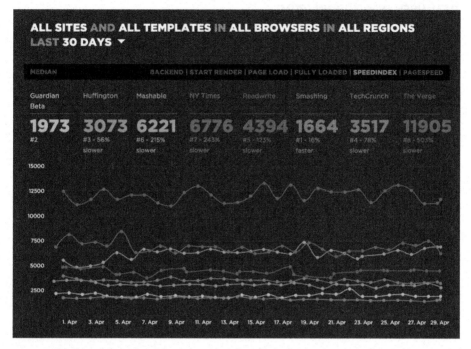

*Figure 4-8. This synthetic benchmark test shows the side-by-side performance of a handful of popular media sites (via SpeedCurve)*

## What synthetic measurement can't tell you

Synthetic measurement can tell you a great deal about how a page is constructed, but there are gaps in what it can tell you:

- Synthetic measurement gives you a series of performance snapshots, not a complete performance picture. Synthetic tests are periodic, not ongoing, so you can miss changes and events that happen between tests.

- Because you have to script all your tests, you're limited by the number of paths you can measure. Most site owners only look at a handful of common user paths.

- Synthetic tests can't identify isolated or situational performance issues (i.e., they cannot pinpoint how your performance is affected by traffic spikes or short-term third-party outages and slowdowns).

## REAL USER MONITORING (RUM)

Real user monitoring is a form of passive monitoring that "listens" to all your traffic as users move through your site. Because RUM never sleeps, it gathers data from every user using every browser across every network, anywhere in the world. We're talking about petabytes of data collected over billions of page views,

The word "passive" is a misnomer, because modern RUM is anything but passive. Today, the best RUM tools have powerful analytics engines that allow you to slice and dice your data in endless ways.

RUM technology collects your website's performance metrics directly from the browser of your end user. You embed a JavaScript beacon in your web pages. This beacon gathers data from each person who visits that page and sends this data back to you to analyze in any number of ways.

### What real user monitoring can tell you

In addition to the usual page metrics, such as load time, real user monitoring can teach you a great deal about how people use your site, uncovering insights that would otherwise be impossible to obtain.

Here are just a few questions your RUM data can answer:

- How is your site affected by traffic surges? Does performance degrade over time?
- What are your users' environments? What kind of browser, device, and operating system are they using to visit your site?
- How do users move through your site? Visitors rarely travel in a straightforward line. Real user monitoring lets you measure performance for every permutation of a navigational path an end user might take through your website (Figure 4-9).
- How are your third-party scripts performing in realtime?
- What impact does website performance have on your actual business? RUM lets you connect the dots between website performance and UX/ business metrics such as bounce rate, page views, time on site, conversion rate, and revenue. It can also show you which pages on your site are most affected by performance slowdowns, giving you guidance as to where to focus your optimization efforts.

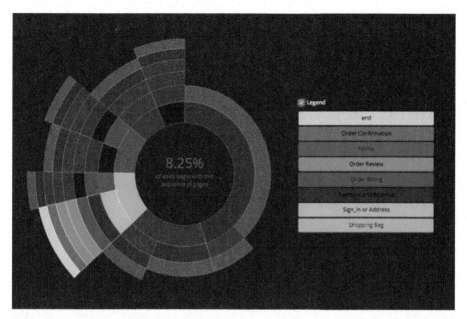

*Figure 4-9. This sunburst chart, created using RUM data, depicts common user paths through a website (via SOASTA mPulse)*

## What real user monitoring can't tell you

Just as synthetic measurement has its strengths and weaknesses, so does RUM:

- Because of the way RUM is implemented (with JavaScript beacons embedded in your pages), it can't measure your competitors' sites and benchmark your performance against theirs.

- RUM is deployed on live sites, so it can't measure performance on your pages when they're in pre-production.

- While RUM does offer some page diagnostics, many tools today don't take a deep dive into analyzing performance issues.

---

**TL;DR**

There is no such thing as an average user. Every user experience is different. And every site delivers both great and terrible user experiences to users every day.

Real user monitoring measures the broad spectrum of user experiences. Synthetic performance tests give you snapshots of user experiences within very specific parameters. Understanding what each type of performance measurement tool can help you with is the key to using each to its best advantage.

---

## Will Browser Evolution Save Us?

I'd be remiss if I left this chapter without touching on browser performance. Throughout the entire history of the World Wide Web, developers have been chugging away in the background, building the most essential app of all—the browser—without which none of us would be able to access the Internet as we know it.

Being a browser developer is thankless work. When we have slow online experiences, we tend to curse the sites we visit, the networks we use, and our poor, hard-working browsers. Yet it's arguable that browser evolution has done more than any other technology to mitigate the performance impact caused by badly designed, poorly optimized sites. (Let's not forget that our comrades at Google were pioneering performance best practices when this issue was just a glimmer on the horizon for most of us.)

From at least the mid-2000s, browser vendors have factored performance into every new release, with the focus on performance becoming stronger with every year.

More recently, web browsers have been getting some pretty major performance upgrades, such as:

*W3C Beacon API*

Deploying beacons on a page can be problematic. The amount of data that can be transferred is severely limited, or the act of sending it can have negative impact on performance. With the new Beacon API, which is supported by most browsers, data can be posted to the server during the browser's unload event in a performant manner, without blocking the browser.

*HTTP/2*

Leading browsers support HTTP/2, which offers a number of performance enhancements, such as multiplexing and concurrency (several requests can be sent in rapid succession on the same TCP connection, and responses can be received out of order); stream dependencies (the client can indicate to the server which resources are most important); and server push (the server can send resources the client has not yet requested).

*Service Workers*

A Service Worker is a script that is run by your browser in the background, separate from a web page, opening the door to features that don't need a web page or user interaction. There are countless great ways to deploy Service Workers to provide performance enhancements—for example, prefetching resources that the user is likely to need in the near future, such as product images from the next pages in a transaction path on an ecommerce site.

The W3C's Web Performance Working Group has also created a substantial handful of real user monitoring specifications (e.g., navigation timing, resource timing, user timing) for in-browser performance diagnostics. This gives site owners the unprecedented ability to gather much more refined and nuanced performance measurements based on actual user behavior.

Individually, each of these enhancements solves a meaningful performance problem. Collectively, these browser enhancements have the potential to fundamentally move the needle on performance in a way that hasn't been seen in years.

## Takeaway

Most people have a basic understanding of Moore's law: the observation that computer processing power doubles roughly every two years. Fewer people are familiar with Wirth's law, which states that software is getting slower more rapidly than hardware is getting faster.

Wirth's law was coined back in 1995, but it's a fairly accurate summary of the web performance conundrum. Regardless of how much money we invest in building out the infrastructure of the Internet, latency will continue—well into the foreseeable future—to be one of the greatest obstacles to optimal web performance. This is due to a couple of issues:

- Rampant increases in page size and complexity.
- For every potentially performance-leeching content type that we see fall out of use (e.g., Flash), a new one rises to take its place (e.g., third-party scripts). And the new one has the potential to be an even worse performance problem than the one it displaces.

Web pages are not likely to become smaller and less complex, so it's fortunate that a huge—and rapidly growing—industry has grown out of the need for making pages more performant.

# 5

# The Future of Performance

If I've done my job right, then by this point you understand that, as Internet users, our performance expectations are understandable and hardwired. You're a convert to the idea that performance correlates to a host of user experience and business metrics. And you have a pretty good awareness of the most common performance bad guys, as well as the various technologies we've developed to fight them.

In this final chapter, we're going to explore some of the emerging issues and questions in the performance space, including the following:

- How can we better understand the intersection between performance, user experience, and business metrics?

- What impact does web performance have on customer lifetime value (CLV)?

- Are we optimizing the right pages?

- Are we always measuring the right things?

- How fast is fast enough?

- How can I create a culture of performance throughout my organization?

## How Can We Better Understand the Intersection Between Performance, User Experience, and Business Metrics?

Businesses need to continuously deliver seamless online experiences, but continuously delivering seamless online experiences is hard. The sheer number and diversity of devices being used today is mind-boggling, and customers expect perfect experiences on every single one of those devices, 24 hours a day.

To meet these relentless expectations, you need to see, understand, and optimize every single user action. Historically, we've had application performance management (APM) tools that measure the health of your site, at both the frontend and the backend. We've had tools that measure customer satisfaction. And we've had tools that measure business performance. What's been missing is the ability to get these tools to speak to each other.

There's a growing understanding that APM is not enough. Out of this, there's an emerging set of practices—which encompass business and IT—that is being called digital performance management by some (though given how much our industry loves acronyms, who knows what we could be calling it in the next few years). As industry commentator Jason Bloomberg wrote, "the current enterprise digital technology market is firing on all cylinders as companies rush to build out their mobile offerings as part of broader digital transformation efforts."[1]

DPM is being touted by analysts as "an evolutionary next step beyond APM."[2] This isn't to say that APM is going away. It should be one of the pillars of a solid performance management platform, alongside all the monitoring and measurement tools that allow you to understand the relationship between performance, user happiness, and ultimately your business. These components include:

- Performance testing solutions that can be deployed continuously to ensure availability

---

1 Jason Bloomberg, "Digital Performance Management Market Heats Up With Dynatrace/Keynote Merger," Forbes, June 17, 2015.

2 Milan Hanson and James McCormick, "Take Application Performance to the Next Level with Digital Performance Management," Forrester Research, February 19, 2016.

- APM/synthetic measurement solutions that benchmark you against your competitors, compare current deployments to previous ones, and offer in-page diagnostics
- Real user monitoring (RUM) solutions that gather data, in real time, about 100% of your user experiences
- Performance analytics tools that slice and dice the data from all your testing, measurement, and monitoring solutions

---

*Digital performance management is APM with a companywide perspective. It goes beyond APM by managing performance in a customer and business context.*

**—MILAN HANSON AND JAMES MCCORMICK,**
**FORRESTER RESEARCH**

---

## What Impact Does Web Performance Have on Customer Lifetime Value?

This is an extension of the previous section, but it's a big enough question that it deserves to be called out in its own right.

In the performance measurement space, the user experience is measured in single sessions, but that's a short-sighted way of looking at things. In the marketing world, marketers take a big-picture look at the entire customer relationship. Typically, customer lifetime value (CLV) is calculated over three years: that's the length of the relationship that marketers expect a customer to have with their brand. So when marketing calculates the ROI for bringing in a new customer, they look at the amount of revenue that customer brings in over the entire relationship.

The web performance community needs to align its customer experience (CX) metrics with marketing's CX metrics. Rather than focusing solely on single user sessions, it would be incredibly helpful to gather and analyze performance data over a much longer window of time. With this data, we can answer questions such as:

- What is the short-term impact of performance improvements or slow-downs on business metrics? What's the long-term impact?

- Do returning visitors have higher or lower performance expectations (evidenced in their willingness to endure poor performance in order to complete a transaction) than first-time visitors?

- Can performance issues be tagged as a contributor to the end of a customer's relationship with a site?

## Are Site Owners Optimizing the Right Pages?

*We worked to make our home page and other key pages faster, and it didn't affect our business.*

One reason why companies work hard to optimize key pages and yet still don't see results: they're optimizing the wrong pages.

Not all web pages are created equal. When pages get slower, conversion rates suffer, but some types of pages suffer more than others. People react differently to slowdowns on different pages in the conversion funnel, which means you need to approach each page differently. While it would be wonderful if we could optimize every single page of our websites, most site owners have only a finite amount of optimization resources. You need to focus those resources on optimizing the pages that matter most to your bottom line.

A new metric, called the conversion impact score, helps identify those pages. Conversion impact scoring uses a site's own real user data, gathered via an RUM solution, to answer the question: what's the relative impact of load time changes on business performance per page?

In Figure 5-1, you can see the conversion impact scores and load times for a set of pages on a site. The blue bars represent the conversion impact score for each page, and the green line represents the median page load time for each page. The pages are ranked from those with the highest conversion impact scores (such as product and category pages; in other words, pages viewed in the "browse" phase of the conversion funnel) to pages with the lowest scores (such as sign-in and account pages).

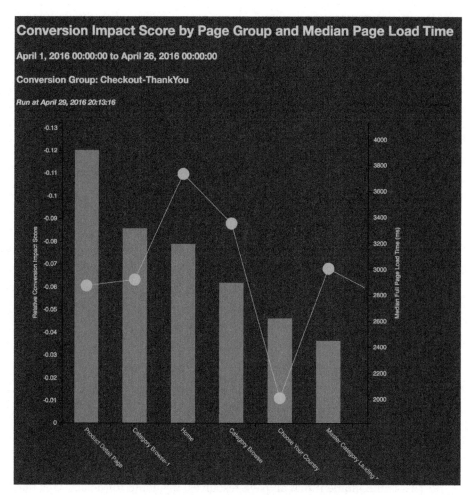

*Figure 5-1. Conversion impact scores (blue bars) and load times (green line) for page groups on a site (while the page groups with the highest conversion impact scores have relatively good load times, their scores indicate that they're the best candidates for further performance optimization)*

The conversion impact score is just one new metric for delivering faster, more successful pages. The performance industry needs to correlate load time with other metrics that are meaningful to your business, and develop more tools that can weight your results so that site owners know what pages to tackle first to get the best ROI for their optimization efforts.

(For nonecommerce sites, there's a companion metric—the activity impact score—which answers the question: what's the relative impact of load time differences on a site's bounce rate?)

## Are We Measuring the Right Things?

Most site owners are not measuring the user experience accurately. This isn't a criticism—it's an open acknowledgment that capturing the exact moment that a page becomes usable is tricky.

Historically, most measurement tools have focused on these three timing metrics:

*Start render*

Indicates when content *begins* to display in the user's browser. Start render is an important metric for measuring the user experience, because it lets you know how long your visitor is staring at a blank screen, but it's not a standalone metric. It's important to note that start render doesn't indicate whether the first content to populate the browser is useful or important, or simply ads and widgets.

*Document complete*

The time it takes for most page resources to render in the browser. It's measured when the browser fires something called an "onLoad event" after most page resources have fully loaded. It's used as a primary measuring stick for site performance, but it isn't necessarily an accurate indicator of when a page initially becomes interactive.

*Fully loaded*

This is the moment that all page resources, including third-party tags that aren't visible, have loaded and the page is complete.

While each of these metrics has its uses, none are a reliable measure of when a page becomes interactive. That's because interactivity varies from page to page and in the past has been challenging to tool.

The Speed Index metric is a useful metric that was added to WebPagetest in 2012. It was created to meet the need for a synthetic metric that could, as much as possible, measure user-perceived performance. The Speed Index measures how quickly a page's visual content renders in the browser and computes an overall score based on the average time, in milliseconds, that it took for the content to appear (the lower the score, the better). This score is useful for comparing experiences of pages against each other (e.g., before and after optimizing, benchmarking against competitors). It's intended to be used in conjunction with metrics like load time and start render, in order to better understand a site's performance.

User Timing is an emerging metric for gathering much more specific real user data around how pages render and how we measure user satisfaction and other business metrics.[3] User Timing is a great way to log your performance metrics into a standardized interface. At a practical level, what this lets you do is measure the render time of specific page assets that are notorious performance leeches (e.g., stylesheets, synchronous scripts, custom fonts, and hero images), and ultimately get a much more specific and nuanced understanding of the real end user experience.[4]

As more services and browsers support User Timing (right now it's supported by 69% of browsers), you'll be able to see your User Timing data in more and more places. Currently less than 10% of leading retail sites have adopted User Timing. This is a great opportunity to get ahead of the curve.

## How Fast Is Fast Enough?

As a staunch user experience advocate for two decades, I find it extremely weird to even find myself saying this, but sometimes it's OK not to deliver the very fastest user experience.

Yes, there's the idealistic, altruistic argument that we should serve the best, fastest user experience to all visitors. But sometimes you have to make a "Sophie's choice" about where to invest your limited resources. You need data to help drive those hard choices:

- What does "faster" mean?
- Who defines "fast" within an organization?
- How do you know when the site or app you're building has achieved mythical "fast enough" status?

---

3  User Timing Recommendation, W3C, December 12, 2013.

4  Steve Souders, "User Timing and Custom Metrics," SpeedCurve Blog, November 12, 2015.

The only way to answer the question "How fast is fast enough?" is to come up with a set of metrics for "fast enough" that work for your company and your visitors. Here's a quick guide to getting started.

## STEP 1: MEASURE

There are scores of case studies (some of which are covered earlier in this book) about the impact of performance on business and user experience metrics. I love these case studies because they shine tons of light on the business value of performance. But none of these case studies shine light on *your* website and *your* visitors. That's why you need to collect and analyze your own site and user data.

There are a number of synthetic and real user monitoring tools—both paid and open source—available. Some of the free tools include WebPagetest, boomerang.js, PhantomJS, Episodes, YSlow, and sitespeed.io.

## STEP 2: CORRELATE

Next, you need to graph the correlation between load time and whatever business/user experience metrics are relevant to your business. These can include bounce rate, conversion rate, revenue, order value, and time on site, to name just a few.

The sample histogram in Figure 5-2 shows the distribution of converted users across load times. It also shows the conversion rate for each cohort of users who experienced each load time.

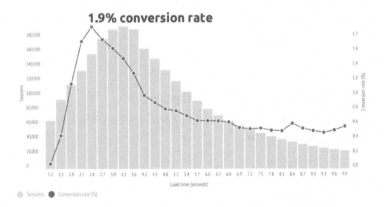

*Figure 5-2. Graph depicting the correlation of load time and conversion rate for a retail website*

Using this graph, it's easy to connect the dots and define the performance sweet spot. For example, if your goal is to convert roughly 2% of your site's traffic, then your performance sweet spot is between 2.1 and 2.7 seconds. The highest conversion rate—1.9%—correlates with an average load time of 2.5 seconds.

If this were your site's data, you could then create a target: all pages must load in 2.7 seconds or less. You could then set an alert within your real user monitoring tool, which flags every time one of your pages exceeds this target.

This is a very simple example. Your targets and alerts can be much more nuanced than this, if, for example, your test data tells you that some pages and geographies are more sensitive than others to performance issues.

### STEP 3: MONITOR

Your site changes. Your users change. This means your performance sweet spot isn't a fixed target. It will fluctuate. You need to monitor your site and user behavior constantly, noting how correlations change over time and adjusting your targets accordingly.

### STEP 4: OPTIMIZE

It goes without saying (I hope) that diagnosing and fixing performance issues, as well as identifying opportunities to apply aggressive new frontend optimizations, is part of the "getting to fast enough" cycle.

### STEP 5: REPEAT

Years ago, someone told me that optimizing performance is like painting the Golden Gate Bridge: it never ends. While this sounds tedious, it's anything but. Each year brings new and constantly evolving tools and best practices. There's always more to learn and exciting ways to innovate.

## How to Create a Culture of Performance in Your Business

*First and foremost, we believe that speed is more than a feature. Speed is the most important feature.*

**—FRED WILSON, UNION SQUARE VENTURES**

It seems fitting to end with this section. I hope that, after reading this book, you warmly embrace the importance of web performance for your business. The next step is to share this knowledge with others and create performance advocates in every corner of your business.

In her excellent book, *Designing for Performance* (O'Reilly), Lara Hogan dedicates an entire chapter to the subject of how to change the performance culture at your organization—from C-suite to developers and designers. In her book, and elsewhere, she offers excellent tips for creating widespread awareness of performance.

## BUILD YOUR CASE

Use relevant case studies—or better yet, your own data—to demonstrate the value of performance to your coworkers and executive team.

## BENCHMARK YOUR SITE

Measure how fast you currently are. You can use this as a yardstick to compare your current performance to future changes. You can also use synthetic measurement tools to benchmark yourself against your competitors. WebPagetest gives you the ability to generate side-by-side videos that show your site rendering alongside competing home pages. (I've found these to be very motivating when talking with executives.)

## COMMUNICATE YOUR PERFORMANCE GOALS

Set performance targets, make them visible and persistent throughout your company, and hold your team accountable to them.

It's becoming common practice for performance-conscious sites to set specific internal service-level agreements. Here's a good example of a specific, measurable, realistic SLA:

*The homepage of our site will load in under 3 seconds measured at the 80th percentile via synthetic tests running in New York, LA, Seattle, and Miami every 30 minutes. We will measure this SLA at 8:00am every morning and base it off the last 24 hours of data.*[5]

Another common communication practice is for companies to display performance dashboards in open areas within their offices.[6] This is a great way to keep performance top of mind for people who might not otherwise consider it an issue that touches their day-to-day work.

---

5 Jonathan Klein, "How Fast Is Your Website? Setting (and Keeping) Web Performance SLAs," Yottaa Blog, July 19, 2011.

6 Lara Hogan, "Performance: Showing Versus Telling," A List Apart, July 14, 2015.

### IDENTIFY PERFORMANCE CHAMPIONS WITHIN YOUR COMPANY

Everyone who touches a web page—from people on the business side, looking to add third-party analytics tags, to folks on the marketing team, wanting to add high-resolution hero images—needs to know that their decisions affect performance. You need to cultivate performance "cops" and "janitors" (to use Lara Hogan's words) throughout your company.

## Takeaway

*Remember that performance is a journey, not a destination.*

The performance arena is littered with case studies about companies that took on performance optimization as a one-off project, experienced short-term benefits, then moved on to other projects and lost all the ground—and gains— they had achieved.

Your site is an organic entity that needs constant care and feeding to stay performant. My greatest hope in writing this book is that I've helped motivate you to embrace performance as an evergreen project, to enjoy the thrill of seeking out innovative fixes for new performance challenges, and to celebrate the impact of performance wins on your business.

# Index

# Get even more for your money.

## Join the O'Reilly Community, and register the O'Reilly books you own. It's free, and you'll get:

- $4.99 ebook upgrade offer
- 40% upgrade offer on O'Reilly print books
- Membership discounts on books and events
- Free lifetime updates to ebooks and videos
- Multiple ebook formats, DRM FREE
- Participation in the O'Reilly community
- Newsletters
- Account management
- 100% Satisfaction Guarantee

### Signing up is easy:

1. Go to: oreilly.com/go/register
2. Create an O'Reilly login.
3. Provide your address.
4. Register your books.

Note: English-language books only

**To order books online:**
oreilly.com/store

**For questions about products or an order:**
orders@oreilly.com

**To sign up to get topic-specific email announcements and/or news about upcoming books, conferences, special offers, and new technologies:**
elists@oreilly.com

**For technical questions about book content:**
booktech@oreilly.com

**To submit new book proposals to our editors:**
proposals@oreilly.com

**O'Reilly books are available in multiple DRM-free ebook formats. For more information:**
oreilly.com/ebooks

## O'REILLY®

# Have it your way.

CPSIA information can be obtained
at www.ICGtesting.com
Printed in the USA
BVOW11s0737020616

450248BV00002B/4/P